HIGHER

GERMAN
2008-2012

BrightRED
PUBLISHING

© Scottish Qualifications Authority
All rights reserved. Copying prohibited. No part of this publication may be reproduced, stored in a retrieval system, or transmitted in any form or by any means, electronic, mechanical, photocopying, recording or otherwise.

First exam published in 2008.
Published by Bright Red Publishing Ltd, 6 Stafford Street, Edinburgh EH3 7AU
tel: 0131 220 5804 fax: 0131 220 6710 info@brightredpublishing.co.uk www.brightredpublishing.co.uk

ISBN 978-1-84948-289-9

A CIP Catalogue record for this book is available from the British Library.

Bright Red Publishing is grateful to the copyright holders, as credited on the final page of the Question Section, for permission to use their material. Every effort has been made to trace the copyright holders and to obtain their permission for the use of copyright material. Bright Red Publishing will be happy to receive information allowing us to rectify any error or omission in future editions.

HIGHER

2008

[BLANK PAGE]

X060/301

NATIONAL
QUALIFICATIONS
2008

THURSDAY, 5 JUNE
9.00 AM – 10.40 AM

GERMAN
HIGHER
Reading and
Directed Writing

45 marks are allocated to this paper. The value attached to each question is shown after each question.

You should spend approximately one hour on Section I and 40 minutes on Section II.

You may use a German dictionary.

SECTION I—READING

Read this magazine article carefully then answer **in English** the questions which follow it.

This article is about a German girl, Sabrina Sadowski, who is spending a year in the United States as an au pair, living and working in a family.

Zwischen Abenteuer und Wahnsinn

Viele Jugendliche beenden ihre Schulzeit und fragen sich, was sie in Zukunft machen sollen. Studium oder Ausbildung?—wenn studieren, was studieren? Zu Hause bleiben
5 oder ausziehen?—wenn ausziehen, wohin denn? Und einige haben vielleicht gar keine Lust, sofort von der Schule an die Uni zu gehen. Wer würde sich da nicht noch ein Jahr Auszeit wünschen, um sich darüber klar
10 zu werden, was man genau will.

Vor einem Jahr ging es mir nicht anders. Deshalb war mir relativ schnell klar: Ich gehe als Au-pair in die Staaten! Es war die beste Entscheidung, die ich je gemacht habe.
15 Natürlich habe ich Horrorgeschichten über versklavte Au-pairs gehört, aber trotzdem stand ich irgendwann am Flughafen.

Das war vor elf Monaten. Ich habe in dieser Zeit wunderbare Menschen kennen
20 gelernt, zahlreiche neue Dinge erlebt und bin viel selbständiger geworden. Ich habe auch mein Englisch auf ein hohes Niveau bringen können.

Während des Au-pair-Jahres in den Staaten
25 muss man je nach Programm sechs bis zwölf „Credits" sammeln. Diese bekommt man durch einen Collegebesuch, Freiwilligenarbeit oder durch Sprachkurse. Ich zum Beispiel habe einen Erste-Hilfe- und einen
30 Spanischkursus abgeschlossen.

In meiner Familie bin ich für zwei Schulkinder verantwortlich. Daher habe ich jeden Morgen frei. Am Nachmittag bin ich hauptsächlich dazu da, die Kinder zur
35 richtigen Zeit an den richtigen Ort zu bringen und ihnen am Abend etwas zu kochen. Jedes Wochenende und jeden Abend habe ich frei. Unter der Woche treffe ich mich meistens mit Freunden in Cafés,
40 zum Videoabend oder in einer Karaokebar. Am Wochenende erkunden wir New York. Ich lebe mit meiner Gastfamilie in New Jersey. Nach einer knappen Stunde Zugfahrt stehe ich mitten auf dem Broadway in
45 Manhattan.

Aber die Geschichten von Horrorfamilien sind leider nicht alle falsch. So kann es passieren, dass ihr in eine Familie mit zwei hyperaktiven Kindern geratet oder dass eine unfreundliche, junge Leute hassende Oma 50 mit im Haus wohnt. Dass ihr jeden Abend bis 22 Uhr arbeiten müsst, oder dass ihr im Kühlschrank nur bestimmte Dinge essen dürft. Wenn ihr dann abends total fertig, unglücklich und müde in euer Bett fallt, 55 welches sich in einem winzigen Raum unter der Treppe befindet, dann werdet ihr euch doch fragen, wieso ihr dieses Leben mit eurem geliebten Zuhause getauscht habt.

Eine Freundin von mir arbeitet bei einer 60 Familie, wo die Eltern mit ihren Kindern so wenig wie möglich zu tun haben wollen. Jeden Morgen muss sie als erste Aufgabe dem achtjährigen Sohn 70 Tabletten geben und danach das Kind zum Psychiater fahren. 65 Laut dem Psychiater sind die Tabletten nichts als Vitamine!

Es ist fast unmöglich, die „perfekte" Familie zu finden. Hier und da muss man sich anpassen und Regeln akzeptieren. Viele 70 Au-pairs haben unter der Woche „Ausgangssperre". Manche müssen schon um 22 Uhr zu Hause sein. Andere können die ganze Nacht wegbleiben, solange sie am nächsten Morgen wieder da sind, um die 75 Kinder zu wecken.

Familien hier sind so unterschiedlich wie in Deutschland auch. Um die passende Familie zu finden, ist es sinnvoll, so ehrlich wie möglich zu sein und sich ganz genau zu 80 überlegen, was man von dem Jahr erwartet. Bei dem telefonischen Interview mit den Familien hat man die Chance, alle möglichen Fragen zu stellen. Man muss nicht unbedingt für Kinder schwärmen, aber 85 hassen sollte man sie auch nicht gerade.

Ich jedenfalls würde jedem ein solches Jahr empfehlen. Wenn man sich nach dem Motto „Was mich nicht umbringt, macht mich stärker!" in den Flieger setzt, kann kaum 90 etwas schief gehen, und man kann sich auf ein tolles Jahr freuen. Neue Erfahrungen sind zumindest garantiert—positive wie negative.

QUESTIONS

Marks

1. According to paragraph one, what questions might young people ask themselves at the end of their school career? **2 points**

2. Read lines 11–23.

   (*a*) How does Sabrina feel about her choice of going to America as an au pair? **1 point**

   (*b*) Eleven months on, what has been good about the experience?

   Mention **two** things. **2 points**

3. Read lines 24–30.

   (*a*) What can au pairs do to collect the credits required by their programmes?

   Mention **two** things. **1 point**

   (*b*) What has Sabrina chosen? **1 point**

4. Now read lines 31–45.

   (*a*) How does she spend her free time during the week? **1 point**

   (*b*) How is it easy for her to explore New York at the weekend? **1 point**

5. Read lines 46–59.

   (*a*) Some au pairs have unpleasant experiences. Give details of **three** of these. **3 points**

   (*b*) What unpleasant accommodation are some au pairs given? **1 point**

6. Read lines 60–67.

   (*a*) What does she say about the parents her friend worked for? **1 point**

   (*b*) What did her friend have to do each day? **1 point**

7. Read lines 68–76.

   Give details of some of the different rules which au pairs must accept. **2 points**

8. Read lines 77–86.

   What advice does the author give about finding a suitable family? **1 point**

9. Read lines 87–94.

   Why should the au pair adopt the motto "what doesn't kill me will make me stronger"? **2 points**

   (20 points)

   = 20 marks

10. Translate into English:

    „In meiner Familie . . . etwas zu kochen." (lines 31–37) **10**

    (30)

[**Turn over for SECTION II on** *Page four*

SECTION II—DIRECTED WRITING

Marks

Last summer your parents arranged a house exchange with a German family.

On your return to Scotland, you are asked to write a report **in German** for the website through which the exchange was arranged.

You must include the following information and **you should try to add** other relevant details:

* how you travelled to the house in Germany **and** how you found the journey

* where exactly the house was situated **and** what it was like, compared with your own home

* what your daily routine was, while you were there

* what you did for food throughout your visit

* a family day-trip you went on, while you were in Germany

* whether your family would like to have another house-exchange and why/why not.

Your report should be 150 – 180 words in length.

Marks will be deducted for any area of information that is omitted.   **(15)**

[END OF QUESTION PAPER]

X060/303

NATIONAL
QUALIFICATIONS
2008

THURSDAY, 5 JUNE
11.00 AM – 12.00 NOON

GERMAN
HIGHER
Listening Transcript

This paper must not be seen by any candidate.

The material overleaf is provided for use in an emergency only (eg the recording or equipment proving faulty) or where permission has been given in advance by SQA for the material to be read to candidates with additional support needs. The material must be read exactly as printed.

Instructions to reader(s):

The dialogue below should be read in approximately 5 minutes. On completion of the first reading, pause for two minutes, then read the dialogue a second time.

Where special arrangements have been agreed in advance to allow the reading of the material, those sections marked **(m)** should be read by a male speaker and those marked **(f)** by a female.

Candidates have two minutes to study the questions before the transcript is read.

Steffi, a 20 year-old German who is spending a year in Scotland, talks about earlier trips she has made here.

(m)   **Hatten deine Eltern nichts dagegen, dass du ohne sie nach Schottland fliegst?**

(f)   Ich bin schon einmal ohne meine Eltern weggefahren. Das hat wunderbar geklappt! Ich glaube, dass meine Eltern mir deshalb bei dieser Reise noch mehr vertrauen!

(m)   **Was sind die Vorteile, wenn man ohne Eltern wegfährt?**

(f)   Wenn ich ohne Eltern verreise, bin ich viel freier. Ich kann also mit meinen Freunden bis 3 Uhr morgens feiern gehen und niemand meckert darüber!

Wir konnten auch immer ausschlafen und dann einfach das anschauen, worauf wir Lust hatten.

(m)   **Woher hast du das Geld für die Reise bekommen?**

(f)   Ich kriege oft Geld von meinen Verwandten zu meinem Geburtstag. Davon habe ich etwas gespart. Aber ungefähr die Hälfte des Geldes habe ich von meinen Eltern bekommen.

(m)   **Was musstest du vor der Abfahrt alles organisieren?**

(f)   Wir mussten natürlich die Flüge buchen und dann noch den Bus zum Flughafen reservieren. Um die Unterkunft haben wir uns auch noch gekümmert. Wir haben uns eine schöne, zentral gelegene Jugendherberge ausgesucht und diese dann im Internet gebucht.

(m)   **Wie bist du nach Schottland gereist?**

(f)   Ich habe mich mit meinen Freunden am Hamburger Hauptbahnhof getroffen. Dann sind wir zusammen mit dem Bus zum Flughafen gefahren. Danach sind wir von Hamburg nach Glasgow geflogen.

(m)   **Gab es irgendwelche Zwischenfälle, als ihr unterwegs wart?**

(f)   Schon in Hamburg fing der Ärger an! Unser Flugzeug konnte aufgrund des dichten Nebels nicht pünktlich starten. Wir mussten circa eine Stunde warten! Einer meiner Freunde, Thomas, hat am Flughafen auch noch sein Portemonnaie verloren!

(m)   **Hattet ihr Probleme mit der Unterkunft?**

(f)   Wir hatten ja ein Zimmer für uns fünf gebucht. Aber als wir in unserer Jugendherberge ankamen, sagten sie uns, dass so ein Zimmer nicht mehr frei wäre. Wir haben jedoch ganz schnell eine neue, schöne Jugendherberge gefunden.

(m)   **Gab es Freizeitmöglichkeiten in der Jugendherberge?**

(f)   Es gab einen großen Billardraum und im Wohnzimmer gab es viele Spiele und Bücher, die man benutzen konnte. Im kleinen Garten stand sogar ein Grill. Wenn es nicht geregnet hat, haben wir einen gemütlichen Abend draußen verbracht.

(m) **Was hast du alles in Glasgow unternommen?**

(f) In Glasgow haben wir uns zum Beispiel die Kunstgalerie angesehen. Einkaufen waren wir natürlich auch, die Innenstadt hat ja so viele Geschäfte! Außerdem gibt es in Glasgow eine so große Auswahl an Klubs und Kneipen.

(m) **Warst du nur in Glasgow?**

(f) Nein, nach ein paar Tagen in Glasgow sind wir nach Edinburgh gefahren. Wir haben uns die bekannte Burg angeschaut und sind die Princes Street entlang geschlendert. Dann führte uns unsere Reise in den Norden. Es ging nach Fort William und dort sind wir wandern gegangen.

(m) **Würdest du Schottland als Reiseziel empfehlen?**

(f) Schottland ist auf jeden Fall eine Reise wert. Die Städte haben ein reiches Kulturangebot, ein aufregendes Nachtleben und sehr gute Einkaufsmöglichkeiten! Gleichzeitig kann man in Schottland eine wunderbare Natur erleben—die vielen Seen und das Hochland sind sehr sehenswert.

(m) **Warst du zum ersten Mal in Großbritannien?**

(f) Nein. In der 7. Klasse sind wir nach Inverness gereist. Unsere Schule in Hamburg und die in Inverness haben ein Austauschprogramm. In einem Jahr kommen die schottischen Schüler nach Hamburg und im nächsten Jahr fliegen die deutschen Jugendlichen nach Inverness. Das ist eine tolle Möglichkeit ein neues Land kennen zu lernen.

(m) **Würdest du eine Auslandserfahrung, wie diese Reise nach Schottland, anderen Jugendlichen weiter empfehlen?**

(f) Ich würde diesen Trip auf jeden Fall weiter empfehlen! Wir haben neue Menschen und eine andere, spannende Kultur kennen gelernt! Es hat uns allen richtig viel Spaß gemacht!

[END OF TRANSCRIPT]

[BLANK PAGE]

FOR OFFICIAL USE

Examiner's Marks	
A	
B	

Total Mark

X060/302

NATIONAL
QUALIFICATIONS
2008

THURSDAY, 5 JUNE
11.00 AM – 12.00 NOON

GERMAN
HIGHER
Listening/Writing

Fill in these boxes and read what is printed below.

Full name of centre

Town

Forename(s)

Surname

Date of birth

Day Month Year   Scottish candidate number   Number of seat

Do not open this paper until told to do so.

Answer Section A **in English** and Section B **in German**.

Section A

Listen carefully to the recording with a view to answering, **in English**, the questions printed in this answer book. Write your answers **clearly and legibly** in the spaces provided after each question.

You will have 2 minutes to study the questions before hearing the dialogue for the first time.

The dialogue will be played **twice**, with an interval of 2 minutes between the two playings.

You may make notes at any time but only in this answer book. **Draw your pen through any notes before you hand in the book.**

Move on to Section B when you have completed Section A: you will **not** be told when to do this.

Section B

Do not write your response in this book: **use the 4 page lined answer sheet**.

You will be told to insert the answer sheet inside this book before handing in your work.

You may consult a German dictionary at any time during **both** sections.

Before leaving the examination room you must give this book to the invigilator. If you do not, you may lose all the marks for this paper.

SA X060/302 6/6170

DO NOT
WRITE
THIS
MARGIN

Section A

Marks

Steffi, a 20 year-old German who is spending a year in Scotland, talks about earlier trips she has made here.

1. What are the advantages of going on holiday without your parents?   **3 points**

2. How **exactly** did she get the money for the holiday?   **2 points**

3. What **three** things did they have to organise before leaving?   **3 points**

4. What went wrong before they even left Hamburg?   **2 points**

5. What difficulty did they have with their accommodation?   **1 point**

DO NOT
WRITE IN
THIS
MARGIN

Marks

6. What facilities did their accommodation have?   **2 points**

7. Why did they enjoy shopping in Glasgow?   **1 point**

8. What did they do in Edinburgh?   **1 point**

9. What does she say about Scotland as a tourist destination? Give **two** details.   **2 points**

10. What information does she give about her first visit to Scotland?   **2 points**

11. Why would Steffi recommend a trip abroad?   **1 point**

(20 points)
= 20 marks

[Turn over for Section B on *Page four*

Marks

Section B

Und du, würdest du mit Freunden, mit der Familie oder alleine verreisen? Welche Art von Urlaub sagt dir zu—zum Beispiel Relaxen am Meer oder durch Europa reisen?

Schreibe 120 – 150 Worte zu diesen Fragen!

10

(30)

USE THE 4 PAGE LINED ANSWER SHEET FOR YOUR ANSWER TO SECTION B

[END OF QUESTION PAPER]

HIGHER

2009

[BLANK PAGE]

X060/301

NATIONAL QUALIFICATIONS 2009	WEDNESDAY, 20 MAY 1.00 PM – 2.40 PM	**GERMAN** HIGHER Reading and Directed Writing

45 marks are allocated to this paper. The value attached to each question is shown after each question.

You should spend approximately one hour on Section I and 40 minutes on Section II.

You may use a German dictionary.

SECTION I—READING

Read the whole of this newspaper article carefully and then answer **in English** the questions which follow it.

Three generations of a German family write about their experiences of summer. Grandmother Ingrid Dehnert (65) and mother Katrin Bredner (43) compare with daughter Carolin (17) how summer was then and what it is like now.

Von Limo zu Tequila Sunrise

Das, was die Menschen am Sommer genießen, scheint sich im Laufe der Zeit nicht geändert zu haben. Sonne, Wärme und Freizeit sind auch für diese drei Frauen die
5 absolut besten Dinge an der sommerlichen Jahreszeit. Wie man die freie Zeit jedoch nutzt, das hat sich mit jeder Generation stark verändert.

Ferienbeschäftigung

10 „Als ich noch jung war, machte ich in der Sommerzeit immer viel mit Freunden zusammen. Wir gingen viel baden, mussten aber immer laufen, da es noch keine Busse gab. Ich arbeitete nebenbei auch als
15 Kindermädchen und verdiente am Tag 50 Pfennige und eine Buttersemmel", berichtet Oma Ingrid Dehnert. „Wir haben auch immer die Touristen von der Fähre abgeholt und ihre Koffer in die Pensionen
20 gefahren. Wir sind aber nie in den Urlaub gefahren, weil wir nicht genug Geld hatten. Meine Mutter sagte oft zu uns Kindern: ‚Ich möchte so gerne einmal mit euch in die Berge fahren . . .!' Sie wollte uns immer die
25 Alpen zeigen."

In der Generation von Mutter Katrin Bredner war es schon anders: „Ich habe ab und zu in der Milchbar gearbeitet, bin sehr viel wandern gegangen, und manchmal sind
30 wir auch in den Urlaub an die Ostsee gefahren."

Tochter Carolin erzählt: „Heute gehen wir viel in die Disco, auf Open-Air-Konzerte, ins Kino und Döner, Pizza oder Eis essen."

35 ### Essen und Trinken

„Egal, wo wir hingegangen sind, wir haben unser Essen mitgenommen. Wenn wir das Geld hatten, haben wir eine Flasche Limonade gekauft, die wir uns geteilt
40 haben", erzählt Oma Ingrid. Die Getränke des Sommers haben sich im Laufe der Zeit stark geändert. Von Limonade bis Cola war es ein langer Weg. Heute stehen

Mixgetränke wie Tequila Sunrise oder Cosmopolitan auf der Getränkekarte. 45

Sommermode

Auch in Sachen Kleidung passierte ein großer Wandel. „Früher hatten wir noch selbst geschneiderte Sachen. Wir trugen in der Regel Kleider und Röcke. Außerdem 50 krempelten wir die Röcke hoch, um Miniröcke zu erhalten. Meine Lieblingsfarbe des Sommers war damals Rot", sagt die Großmutter.

„In unserer Zeit gab es schon Miniröcke, 55 aber auch kurze Hosen. Die Farbe des Sommers war damals Blau", so Katrin Bredner. Carolin Bredner weiß, wie es jetzt aussieht: „Heute sind viele Farben aktuell. Auch Streifen werden oft getragen", sagt sie. 60

Party und Feiern

Neben der Mode sind noch weitere Unterschiede festzustellen. Viele Jugendliche in der heutigen Zeit nutzen die Ferien, um richtig zu feiern. Daran war früher 65 nicht zu denken. In der Generation von Ingrid Dehnert waren die einzigen Feiermöglichkeiten Familienfeste, und selbst dann mussten die Kinder um Mitternacht zu Hause sein. Katrin Bredner dagegen lebt in 70 einer Generation, die in ihrer Jugend schon viel die Disco besuchte. Heute ist es am extremsten. „Wir gehen heute, wenn es klappt, jedes Wochenende in die Disco. Jugendliche besuchen auch Stadtfeste zum 75 Feiern", erklärt Carolin.

Musik und Sommerhits

Die spannendste Verwandlung passierte jedoch bei der Musik. Als Oma Ingrid noch jung war, wurden nur Wanderlieder 80 gesungen. Jedoch in der Generation von Katrin Bredner war das schon ganz anders. Die Jugendlichen nahmen ihre eigenen Stimmen und viel Musik mit einem Kassettenrekorder auf und hörten sich diese 85 an. Heute kommt nahezu kein Jugendlicher ohne MP3-Player oder I-Pod aus.

Fazit

90 Zum Schluss sollen die drei Frauen den Satz „Ich habe den Sommer in meiner Jugend genossen, weil . . .“ fortsetzen.

„. . . weil man Freizeit hat und die Sonne und die Ruhe genießen kann“, antwortet Carolin Bredner. Ihre Mutter Katrin sagt: „. . . weil mir die Sonne sehr wichtig war und 95 man sich entspannen konnte.“ Die Antwort von Oma Ingrid ist jedoch die, die am meisten fasziniert. „Wir waren frei“, sagt sie.

QUESTIONS

Marks

1. (a) Across the three generations, what has **not** changed over the years? — **1 point**

   (b) What has changed a great deal? — **1 point**

2. Read lines 9–34.

   (a) What does grandmother Ingrid Dehnert say about going swimming with friends in summer, when she was young? — **1 point**

   (b) Apart from child-minding, what did she do to earn money? — **2 points**

   (c) How did Katrin Bredner spend her holidays? — **2 points**

3. Read lines 35–45.

   In grandmother Ingrid's day, what did they do for food and drink, when they went out? — **2 points**

4. Now read lines 46–60.

   (a) What sort of clothes did grandmother Ingrid's generation wear in the summer? — **1 point**

   (b) What does Katrin say about clothes in her day? — **1 point**

   (c) What do today's young people wear? — **1 point**

5. Read lines 61–76.

   (a) What are you told about parties, when Ingrid was young? — **2 points**

   (b) How do the young people of today like to celebrate? — **2 points**

6. Read lines 77–87.

   What changes in music took place between Oma Ingrid's and Katrin Bredner's generation? — **2 points**

7. Read lines 88–98.

   Why did Katrin enjoy summers, when she was a girl? — **2 points**

   (20 points)

   = 20 marks

8. Translate into English:

   „Wir sind aber . . . uns immer die Alpen zeigen.“ (lines 20–25) — **10**

   (30)

[Turn over for SECTION II on *Page four*

SECTION II—DIRECTED WRITING

Marks

You have travelled to Germany to spend three months working in a town there.

When you return to Scotland, you have to write a report **in German** for the languages department in your school/college.

You must include the following information and **you should try to add** other relevant details:

- how you travelled to Germany **and** what the town was like
- where your accommodation was situated **and** what it was like
- what your job involved **and** how you got on with the people you worked with
- what you did in your spare time to experience the country/culture
- what you did on your last night before coming home
- why you would/would not recommend working in Germany to others.

Your report should be 150 – 180 words in length.

Marks will be deducted for any area of information that is omitted.   **(15)**

[END OF QUESTION PAPER]

X060/303

NATIONAL
QUALIFICATIONS
2009

WEDNESDAY, 20 MAY
3.00 PM – 4.00 PM

GERMAN
HIGHER
Listening Transcript

This paper must not be seen by any candidate.

The material overleaf is provided for use in an emergency only (eg the recording or equipment proving faulty) or where permission has been given in advance by SQA for the material to be read to candidates with additional support needs. The material must be read exactly as printed.

Instructions to reader(s):

The dialogue below should be read in approximately 3½ minutes. On completion of the first reading, pause for two minutes, then read the dialogue a second time.

Where special arrangements have been agreed in advance to allow the reading of the material, those sections marked **(m)** should be read by a male speaker and those marked **(f)** by a female.

Candidates have two minutes to study the questions before the transcript is read.

Meike, a 20 year-old German from Markersdorf near Görlitz in Saxony, talks about getting a training place.

(m)   **Meike, wo kommst du her und wo wohnst du jetzt?**

(f)   Ich komme aus Markersdorf. Das ist eine Gemeinde in Sachsen mit etwa 4.500 Einwohnern. Jetzt wohne ich in Hamburg, das ist eine Großstadt und liegt etwa 500 km von Görlitz entfernt.

(m)   **Warum bist du nach Hamburg gezogen?**

(f)   Hier in Görlitz gibt es nur relativ wenige Ausbildungsplätze für die vielen Schüler. Für uns gibt es nur eine einzige Alternative. Wir müssen unsere Stadt, Eltern und Freunde verlassen, um in einer anderen Stadt einen Ausbildungsplatz zu bekommen. Deswegen bin ich nach Hamburg gezogen.

(m)   **Wie war das am Anfang?**

(f)   Nicht so einfach. Natürlich habe ich meine Freunde, meine Familie und meine Umgebung vermisst. Am Anfang kennt man ja niemanden. Mittlerweile habe ich schon viele Freunde gefunden.

(m)   **Gibt es Vorteile, wenn man weit weg von zu Hause wohnt?**

(f)   Selbstverständlich! Man kann Freunde mit nach Hause bringen - egal wie spät es ist. Und am Wochenende kann man solange schlafen, wie man will.

(m)   **Gibt es auch Nachteile?**

(f)   Na klar. Man muss alles selbst machen. Das bedeutet, man muss selbst einkaufen, selbst putzen und sich sein Geld einteilen, damit es bis zum Ende des Monats reicht.

(m)   **Wolltest du von zu Hause wegziehen?**

(f)   Eigentlich, ja. Für mich war es eine gute Entscheidung, fortzugehen. Im Vergleich zu meinen alten Klassenkameraden und Freunden, die in Görlitz arbeiten, verdiene ich auch mehr Geld.

(m)   **Wie hast du diese Ausbildungsstelle in Hamburg bekommen?**

(f)   Eigentlich nur durch Zufall! Ein Arbeitskollege ist krank geworden und ich habe seinen Platz bekommen. Ich war recht froh, diese Stelle in Hamburg zu bekommen, weil ich in Norddeutschland leben wollte.

(m)   **Wie ist es mit dem Umzug nach Hamburg gelaufen?**

(f)   Ich hatte das Glück, dass meine Eltern mich beim Umzug sehr unterstützt haben. Sie haben mir sehr viel geholfen. Sie sind mit mir zusammen nach Hamburg gefahren und wir haben eine Wohnung gesucht. Innerhalb von drei Tagen haben sie mit mir alles für die Wohnung gekauft.

(m) **Ist es wirklich ein großer Unterschied, ob man in Hamburg oder in Görlitz lebt?**

(f) Ja, das sowieso. Hamburg ist nicht nur sehr viel größer, die Einwohner sprechen auch einen anderen Dialekt.

(m) **Fährst du noch oft nach Görlitz?**

(f) Nicht so oft. Aber ich bin froh, wenn ich mal wieder zu Hause bin, weil ich dann meine alten Freunde treffen kann.

(m) **War es für dich ein sehr großer Schritt von zu Hause auszuziehen?**

(f) Sicher. Seitdem ich in Hamburg wohne, bin ich auf jeden Fall selbstständiger geworden und vielleicht sogar ein Stück erwachsener.

[END OF TRANSCRIPT]

[BLANK PAGE]

FOR OFFICIAL USE

Examiner's Marks	
A	
B	

Total Mark

X060/302

NATIONAL
QUALIFICATIONS
2009

WEDNESDAY, 20 MAY
3.00 PM – 4.00 PM

GERMAN
HIGHER
Listening/Writing

Fill in these boxes and read what is printed below.

Full name of centre

Town

Forename(s)

Surname

Date of birth

Day Month Year   Scottish candidate number   Number of seat

Do not open this paper until told to do so.

Answer Section A **in English** and Section B **in German**.

Section A

Listen carefully to the recording with a view to answering, **in English**, the questions printed in this answer book. Write your answers **clearly and legibly** in the spaces provided after each question.

You will have 2 minutes to study the questions before hearing the dialogue for the first time.

The dialogue will be played **twice**, with an interval of 2 minutes between the two playings.

You may make notes at any time but only in this answer book. **Score out any notes before you hand in the book.**

Move on to Section B when you have completed Section A: you will **not** be told when to do this.

Section B

Do not write your response in this book: **use the 4 page lined answer sheet**.

You will be told to insert the answer sheet inside this book before handing in your work.

You may consult a German dictionary at any time during **both** sections.

Before leaving the examination room you must give this book to the invigilator. If you do not, you may lose all the marks for this paper.

Section A   *Marks*

Meike, a 20 year-old German from Markersdorf near Görlitz in Saxony, talks about getting a training place.

1.   How many people live in Markersdorf?   **1 point**

2.   (*a*) What does Meike say about the number of training places in Görlitz?   **1 point**

      (*b*) What is the only alternative the young people have?   **1 point**

3.   At the beginning, how did she find living in Hamburg?   **2 points**

4.   What are the advantages of living far away from home?   **2 points**

5.   What are the disadvantages?   **3 points**

6.   Why does she feel that moving away was a good decision?   **1 point**

Marks

7. (*a*) How did Meike get this training place?   **1 point**

    (*b*) Why was she pleased?   **1 point**

8. How did her parents help her with the move to Hamburg?   **3 points**

9. What are the **two** differences between Hamburg and Görlitz?   **2 points**

10. Why does she like to go back to Görlitz?   **1 point**

11. How has she changed since leaving home?   **1 point**

**(20 points)
= 20 marks**

[Turn over for Section B on *Page four*

Marks

Section B

Was meinst du, was sind die Vorteile und Nachteile von deinem Wohnort? Willst du lieber bei den Eltern wohnen oder von Zuhause ausziehen?

Schreibe 120 – 150 Worte zu diesen Fragen!   **10**

(30)

USE THE 4 PAGE LINED ANSWER SHEET FOR YOUR ANSWER TO SECTION B

[END OF QUESTION PAPER]

[BLANK PAGE]

2010

[BLANK PAGE]

X060/301

NATIONAL QUALIFICATIONS 2010	WEDNESDAY, 19 MAY 1.00 PM – 2.40 PM	**GERMAN** HIGHER Reading and Directed Writing

45 marks are allocated to this paper. The value attached to each question is shown after each question.

You should spend approximately one hour on Section I and 40 minutes on Section II.

You may use a German dictionary.

SECTION I—READING

Read the whole of this newspaper article carefully and then answer **in English** the questions which follow it.

Annette leaves Germany to live in Cape Town in South Africa.

Neue Heimat

Von Deutschland nach Südafrika—am Anfang will Annette einfach nur raus aus ihrem Dorf. Irgendwohin. „Ich wollte dahin, wo mich niemand kennt", sagt
5 Annette. „Als Pastorentochter kannst du dich nicht betrinken", sagt sie. „Zumindest nicht, wenn du deinen Eltern nicht peinlich sein möchtest." Annette versteht sich nämlich gut mit ihnen.

10 Sie hat keine Lust auf schlaue Tipps, auf Leute, die ihr erzählen, wie es woanders ist. Sie sucht im Internet, besorgt sich Broschüren, sammelt Informationen über die Arbeit als Au-pair. Und findet dabei eine
15 Vermittlung aus *Kapstadt*: Ein Jahr Südafrika, das ist es!

Aber es geht noch um anderes: „Ich wollte wissen: Wie komme ich allein klar? Wo gehöre ich hin? Wer bin ich?", sagt Annette.
20 Doch die Eltern legen ihr Veto ein. Sie machen sich Sorgen. *Kapstadt*—„Da kann man doch als Frau nicht auf die Straße gehen". Aber je größer der Widerstand, desto entschlossener ist Annette.

25 Sie erinnert sich genau daran, wie sie mit ihren Eltern im Wohnzimmer sitzt: diskutiert, erklärt, protestiert. Schließlich zieht sie den Joker: „Ihr habt mir meine Selbständigkeit beigebracht. Und jetzt wollt
30 ihr mir eine so wichtige Entscheidung aus den Händen nehmen? Ich glaube nicht, dass das richtig ist", sagt sie. Die Eltern schauen sich an. Zehn lange Sekunden. Und unterschreiben das Formular, ohne ein Wort
35 zu sagen. Ihre Tochter hat Recht.

Drei Tage nach dem Abi-Ball geht es los. Als Annette am Flughafen durch die Zollabfertigung geht, dreht sie sich zu ihrer Familie um, winkt und verschwindet. „Jetzt
40 ist sie für immer aus dem Haus", denkt ihr Vater, „die kommt nicht mehr als meine kleine Tochter zurück."

Als sie in *Kapstadt* ankommt, geht es zu den Gasteltern. Alles läuft nach Plan: Die Familie ist nett, mit den beiden Kindern 45 kommt sie klar. Annette macht Frühstück, bringt die Kinder zur Schule. Sie genießt das Leben, geht ins Fitness-Studio, legt sich in die Sonne und liest viel. Nachmittags macht sie den Kindern einen Imbiss und 50 spielt mit ihnen, bis die Eltern kommen. Annette ist froh, weil sie Ruhe hat.

Und dann kommt Karel. Ihr Gastvater hatte seinen Kollegen Karel gebeten, Annette abends in die Clubs mitzunehmen, 55 damit sie das junge *Kapstadt* kennen lernt und sich nicht langweilt. Karel und sie verstehen sich. Sehr sogar. Genau 18 Tage nach dem Kennenlernen will Annette von Karel wissen, was los ist. Ein Kuss und eine 60 Entscheidung. Annette ist erst seit vier Monaten in *Kapstadt*, aber sie weiß: Ich will bleiben. Hier studieren, mit Karel leben.

Im April 2008, kurz vor Ende des Au-pair-Jahres, fliegen Annettes Vater und ihr älterer 65 Bruder nach *Kapstadt*. Sie wollen sich anschauen, wie Annette lebt und wer eigentlich dieser Kerl ist, der alles durcheinander bringt. Karel und Annette sind nervös. Aber die Männer verstehen sich. 70 Alles passt.

Zwei Monate später muss Annette nach Deutschland zurück, um sich für den Studienplatz in *Kapstadt* zu bewerben. Es gibt viele Probleme mit dem Visum, aber ein 75 halbes Jahr später geht der Antrag endlich durch.

<u>Karel kommt über Weihnachten und Silvester nach Deutschland. Als es Zeit für den Rückflug ist, freut sich Annette und ist</u> 80 <u>zugleich sehr traurig. „Ich weiß, dass es für meine Familie schwer ist, aber es ist bestimmt die richtige Entscheidung für mich.</u> Ich wünsche mir nur, dass meine

85 Eltern mich verstehen." Das tun sie, aber natürlich vermissen sie die Tochter, jeden Sonntagabend hängen sie am Telefon.

Letztes Jahr Silvester feierten sie die Hochzeit in Südafrika. Annettes Familie kam 90 eingeflogen. Freunde aus Deutschland feierten fröhlich mit den neuen aus *Kapstadt*.

Es war ein richtig tolles Fest.

Und nun? Wollen beide für immer in *Kapstadt* bleiben? Oder steht irgendwann wieder Deutschland auf dem Lebensplan? 95 „Mal sehen", sagt Annette und grinst. „Wir lassen das offen." Keine Pläne mehr. Sondern: das Leben genießen. Jetzt.

QUESTIONS

Marks

1. Why did Annette first want to leave her village? — **1**

2. Read lines 10–24.

    (*a*) Whose advice was she not interested in? — **1**

    (*b*) How did her parents react to her idea of going to Cape Town? — **2**

3. Read lines 25–35.

    What was the joker she played? — **2**

4. Now read lines 36–42.

    What were her father's thoughts, as she passed through customs at the airport? — **2**

5. Read lines 43–52.

    (*a*) What was Annette's morning routine in Cape Town? Write **four** things. — **2**

    (*b*) What **two** tasks did she have in the afternoons? — **2**

6. Read lines 53–63.

    (*a*) How did Annette come to meet Karel? — **2**

    (*b*) What did she realise four months later? — **1**

7. Read lines 64–71.

    Why did Annette's father and brother fly out to Cape Town in April 2008? — **2**

8. Read lines 72–77.

    Why did Annette have to go back to Germany two months later? — **1**

9. Read lines 88–98.

    Now that Annette and Karel are married, what are their thoughts for the future? — **2**

    (20)

10. Translate into English:

    „Karel kommt . . . die richtige Entscheidung für mich." (lines 78–84) — **10**

    (30)

[Turn over for SECTION II on *Page four*

Marks

SECTION II—DIRECTED WRITING

A German pupil is spending a year at your school/college in Scotland. He/she invited you to go back with him/her to Germany at Easter to spend two weeks with his/her family.

When you return to Scotland, you write **in German** for the languages page of your school/college website.

You must include the following information and **you should try to add** other relevant details:

- how the two of you travelled to Germany **and** what the journey was like

- what the town was like **and** what you thought of the family home

- what you did to help around the home, while you were in Germany

- what you and your German friend did in the afternoons and evenings

- what you liked most/least about the family and the other people you met

- why you would/would not recommend being in Germany just before your Higher exams. **(15)**

Your report should be 150 – 180 words in length.

Marks will be deducted for any area of information that is omitted.

[END OF QUESTION PAPER]

X060/303

NATIONAL
QUALIFICATIONS
2010

WEDNESDAY, 19 MAY
3.00 PM – 4.00 PM

GERMAN
HIGHER
Listening Transcript

This paper must not be seen by any candidate.

The material overleaf is provided for use in an emergency only (eg the recording or equipment proving faulty) or where permission has been given in advance by SQA for the material to be read to candidates with additional support needs. The material must be read exactly as printed.

Instructions to reader(s):

The dialogue below should be read in approximately 3½ minutes. On completion of the first reading, pause for two minutes, then read the dialogue a second time.

Where special arrangements have been agreed in advance to allow the reading of the material, those sections marked **(m)** should be read by a male speaker and those marked **(f)** by a female.

Candidates have two minutes to study the questions before the transcript is read.

Rica, a German girl, talks about getting ready to go to the USA as an exchange student.

(m)   Rica, du fliegst im August in die USA. Seit wann laufen die Vorbereitungen für diese Reise?

(f)   Seit fast einem Jahr. Im Juli 2009 habe ich mich beim Rotary-Club Freital beworben, der diesen Austausch zum Teil finanziert. Nach sechs Wochen habe ich die nötigen Formulare bekommen, um mich anzumelden. Ich musste den Flug buchen und das Visum beantragen.

(m)   Was musst du aus deiner eigenen Tasche bezahlen?

(f)   Den Flug und die Versicherungen müssen wir bezahlen. Ich habe einen Teilzeitjob und habe etwas gespart, den Rest bezahlen meine Eltern.

(m)   Warum ist dein Ziel die USA?

(f)   Wir hatten hier eine Cousine aus den Staaten zu Besuch. Sie hat uns viel über die USA erzählt. Das weckte bei mir das Interesse an dem Land. Aber ich wäre auch in jedes andere Land gegangen. Ich will unbedingt richtig Englisch sprechen lernen.

(m)   Nun ist es dein Wunschland geworden und du willst an einer Highschool lernen. Was begeistert dich so daran?

(f)   Man hört immer so viel davon. Ich will mal sehen, ob dort wirklich alles so ist, wie man es in den Filmen sieht. Ob die Schule in Amerika mehr Spaß macht, als bei uns in Deutschland.

(m)   Dich interessiert nur die Highschool?

(f)   Nein, auch die Landschaft, die kulturellen Unterschiede und die vielen verschiedenen Aspekte des Landes.

(m)   Wohin fliegst du genau?

(f)   Nach Algonquin. Diese Kleinstadt liegt im Staat Illinois und ist ungefähr eine Autostunde von Chicago entfernt. Das Haus meiner Gastfamilie liegt direkt an einem Fluss.

(m)   Wie lange wirst du weg sein?

(f)   Elf Monate. Im August geht es los und im Juli nächsten Jahres komme ich wieder.

(m)   Was sagen deine Freunde und deine Familie zu deinem Austauschjahr?

(f)   Meine Mutter freut sich für mich. Aber es wird schwer für sie sein, wenn ich weg bin. Meine Freunde finden es gut, dass ich diese Möglichkeit habe.

(m)   **Was musst du auf jeden Fall in den Koffer packen?**

(f)   Fotos von meiner Familie und meinen Freunden. Erinnerungsstücke von meiner besten Freundin. Die Klaviernoten, damit ich das Spielen nicht verlerne und deutsche Rezepte von der Oma, darauf kann ich nicht verzichten.

(m)   **Die USA bietet viele Sehenswürdigkeiten. Was willst du nicht verpassen?**

(f)   Auf jeden Fall Chicago. Den Searstower—eines der größten Gebäude der Welt. Und wenn es klappt, fahre ich auch nach New York. Aber das ist ja schon ein ganzes Stück entfernt von Algonquin.

(m)   **Was erhoffst du dir von diesem Auslandsjahr?**

(f)   Ich hoffe, meine Englischkenntnisse verbessern zu können. Außerdem hoffe ich, dass ich nach diesem Jahr selbstbewusster und selbstständiger sein werde.

[*END OF TRANSCRIPT*]

[BLANK PAGE]

FOR OFFICIAL USE

Examiner's Marks	
A	
B	

Total Mark

X060/302

NATIONAL QUALIFICATIONS 2010

WEDNESDAY, 19 MAY 3.00 PM – 4.00 PM

GERMAN HIGHER
Listening/Writing

Fill in these boxes and read what is printed below.

Full name of centre

Town

Forename(s)

Surname

Date of birth

Day   Month   Year   Scottish candidate number   Number of seat

Do not open this paper until told to do so.

Answer Section A **in English** and Section B **in German**.

Section A

Listen carefully to the recording with a view to answering, **in English**, the questions printed in this answer book. Write your answers **clearly and legibly** in the spaces provided after each question.

You will have 2 minutes to study the questions before hearing the dialogue for the first time.

The dialogue will be played **twice**, with an interval of 2 minutes between the two playings.

You may make notes at any time but only in this answer book. **Score out any notes before you hand in the book.**

Move on to Section B when you have completed Section A: you will **not** be told when to do this.

Section B

Do not write your response in this book: **use the 4 page lined answer sheet**.

You will be told to insert the answer sheet inside this book before handing in your work.

You may consult a German dictionary at any time during **both** sections.

Before leaving the examination room you must give this book to the Invigilator. If you do not, you may lose all the marks for this paper.

Marks

Section A

Rica, a German girl, talks about getting ready to go to the USA as an exchange student.

1.   (*a*)   When did Rica first apply to the Rotary Club in Freital?   1

     (*b*)   How long was it before she received the forms she needed?   1

2.   Where is Rica getting the money from to pay for the flight and insurance?   2

3.   Why did Rica choose to go to the United States rather than another English-speaking country?   2

4.   What attracts Rica to go and study at an American high school?   2

5.   Apart from the high school, what interests her? Mention **two** things.   2

6.   Where in Illinois is Algonquin?   1

Marks

7. How long will Rica be away in America?   1

8. (*a*) How is Rica's mother going to feel about her going away to America?   2

    (*b*) What do her friends think about it?   1

9. Give details of the **three** things, other than photos, that Rica is taking with her.   3

10. Why might she not be able to go to New York while she is in America?   1

11. She sees this year as a chance to improve her English. Mention **one** other thing she would like to gain from the year.   1

                                                                               (20)

[Turn over for Section B on *Page four*

Marks

Section B

Was meinst du, möchtest du ein Jahr in einem anderen Land verbringen? Wohin würdest du gehen? Warum?

Schreibe 120 – 150 Worte zu diesen Fragen!   **10**

(30)

USE THE 4 PAGE LINED ANSWER SHEET FOR YOUR ANSWER TO SECTION B

[END OF QUESTION PAPER]

[BLANK PAGE]

X060/301

NATIONAL
QUALIFICATIONS
2011

THURSDAY, 19 MAY
1.00 PM – 2.40 PM

GERMAN
HIGHER
Reading and
Directed Writing

45 marks are allocated to this paper. The value attached to each question is shown after each question.

You should spend approximately one hour on Section I and 40 minutes on Section II.

You may use a German dictionary.

SECTION I—READING

Read the whole of this newspaper article carefully and then answer **in English** the questions which follow it.

Christine Siefer is working during the main tourist season on the small East Friesian island of Juist, where no cars are allowed.

Hinter den Kulissen des Tourismus

Es ist ein typischer sommerlicher Strandtag auf der Ferieninsel *Juist*. Die Urlauber sonnen sich auf dem Platz vor dem *Café Kunststück*. Familien, die gerade vom Strand
5 kommen, gönnen sich ein kühles Getränk und ihren Kindern ein Eis. Mittendrin bin ich, als Kellnerin auf der schönsten Sandbank der Welt.

Ich fühlte mich schon nach wenigen Tagen
10 fast als Insider, die hinter die Kulissen einer Traumwelt schauen darf. Ich habe ein Zimmer in einem Haus, wo auch viele andere Helfer der großen Hotels wohnen. Die Stimmen, die durch die Hinterhöfe schallen,
15 gehören den Menschen, die die Insel als Urlaubsort funktionieren lassen, vom polnischen Zimmermädchen bis hin zum Hotelbesitzer, dessen Familie für den Rest des Jahres von der Arbeit und dem Verdienst
20 der Sommermonate lebt. Die Insel ist nämlich nur 17 Kilometer lang und wenige hundert Meter breit. Ausser in der Urlaubssaison gibt es hier nicht viel Arbeit. Die Kinder müssen auf dem Festland aufs
25 Gymnasium gehen, und die medizinische Versorgung hängt im Notfall von einem Hubschrauber ab.

Das alles interessiert die Urlauber überhaupt nicht. Ihr Ziel ist die Erholung
30 und Entspannung. Dazu tragen der lange weiße Sandstrand und die gute Meeresluft ohne Autoabgase bei.

In meiner ersten Woche war ich die einzige Aushilfskraft im Café, und ich bemerkte bei
35 meinen abendlichen Spaziergängen auf der Promenade ein mir bisher völlig fremdes Gefühl: Einsamkeit. Glücklicherweise folgte bald eine Kollegin im gleichen Alter, und ich fand schnell heraus, dass viele auswärtige
40 Jugendliche auf der Insel arbeiten. So lernte sogar ein Ausgehmuffel wie ich das Nachtleben der Insel kennen. Beim Ausgehen am Abend überraschte es mich sehr, dass die Inselbewohner die gleichen Bars und Kneipen aufsuchen wie die 45 Urlauber. Dort treffen sich dann alle—Bewohner, Besucher und Aushilfskräfte.

Als die Ferien anfingen, blieb das Café zwölf Stunden täglich geöffnet. Von einem Tag auf den anderen war die Insel rappelvoll. 50 Fahrräder, Ziehkoffer und Pferdekutschen, wohin das Auge blickte. Wenn es dann plötzlich mal ein Schauer gibt, wird das Café zum Zufluchtsort Nummer eins. <u>Für uns bedeutet das: Hektik. Bestellungen</u> 55 <u>aufnehmen und servieren, nebenbei den Spülberg in Zaum halten und zwischendurch Geschenke aus dem Souvenirladen einpacken—nach solchen Tagen bin ich abends todmüde ins Bett gefallen.</u> 60

Inzwischen kann ich ein Tablett in der einen und Kuchenteller in der anderen Hand transportieren. In den ersten Wochen sind mir auch manchmal Tassen und Gläser vom Tablett gefallen. Fehler, die die Gäste 65 betrafen, waren mir peinlicher. Ich wollte an einem Tisch kassieren, habe aber nicht auf die Rechnung geschaut. Die Dame stellte sachlich fest, dass sie keine elf Weißbiere getrunken habe und hielt mir den Bon unter 70 die Nase. Ich hatte die Tischnummer verwechselt.

Sehr anstrengend war der Tag, an dem abends eine Rockband auf dem Kurplatz auftrat und die gesamte Insel vor dem Café 75 zusammentraf. Unsere Sitzplätze waren begehrt, und eine Stunde nach der offiziellen Schließung servierten wir weiter. Die meisten Konzertbesucher hatten wenig Verständnis dafür, dass wir endlich schließen wollten. 80 Viele Urlauber verstehen nicht, dass sich eine Servicekraft nach zwölfstündigem Arbeitstag nach dem Feierabend sehnt.

Dennoch: Gerade den Kontakt mit den
85 Gästen nehme ich als die schönste Erfahrung
mit nach Hause. Es ist ein unglaublich gutes
Gefühl, wenn Familien immer wieder ins
Café kommen, ich ihre Bestellung nach
einiger Zeit schon erraten kann und sich
90 nette Gespräche ergeben. Diese positiven

Begegnungen sind häufig und helfen mir,
auch <u>den</u> Feriengästen freundlich zu
begegnen, die keine zehn Minuten auf ihren
Kaffee warten können. Ich werde nie
verstehen können, wie sie zwischen Strand 95
und Hotel diesen Stress aufbauen können.

QUESTIONS

Marks

1. Describe what holiday-makers do on a typical summer's day on the island of Juist.   **3**

2. Read lines 9–27.

   (*a*) With whom does Christine share her accommodation?   **1**

   (*b*) What do you learn about the island of Juist and life there when the summer season is over?   **4**

3. Read lines 28–32.

   What **two** features help holiday-makers relax and recuperate?   **2**

4. Now read lines 33–47.

   (*a*) Why did Christine feel lonely at first?   **1**

   (*b*) How did this change?   **1**

   (*c*) What surprised Christine, when she started to visit the bars and pubs on the island?   **1**

5. Read lines 61–72.

   (*a*) What kind of unfortunate accident did she have in the first weeks of her job?   **1**

   (*b*) What embarrassing mistake did Christine make with one customer?   **1**

6. Read lines 73–83.

   What are Christine's complaints about the people who attended the concert in front of the café?   **2**

7. Read lines 84–96.

   (*a*) What gives Christine a really good feeling, when families keep coming back to the café?   **2**

   (*b*) Which customers do these positive experiences help her to cope with?   **1**

   (20)

8. Translate into English:

   „Für uns . . . ins Bett gefallen." (lines 54–60)   **10**

   (30)

[Turn over for SECTION II on *Page four*

Marks

SECTION II—DIRECTED WRITING

Last October you were invited to travel with a group from your local area to Bavaria to take part in a youth debate together with other young people from Germany and Austria. The debate was about smoking in cafés and restaurants.

When you return to Scotland, you write **in German** for the languages page of your school/college website.

You must include the following information and **you should try to add** other relevant details:

• how your group travelled to Germany **and** what you did during the journey

• what your host family were like **and** what their home was like

• how you got on with the other young people from Germany and Austria

• what you all did in the free time you had

• what you said in the debate and how the debate went

• why you would/would not recommend taking part in an international event like this. **(15)**

Your report should be 150 – 180 words in length.

Marks will be deducted for any area of information that is omitted.

[END OF QUESTION PAPER]

X060/303

NATIONAL QUALIFICATIONS 2011	THURSDAY, 19 MAY 3.00 PM – 4.00 PM	GERMAN HIGHER Listening Transcript

This paper must not be seen by any candidate.

The material overleaf is provided for use in an emergency only (eg the recording or equipment proving faulty) or where permission has been given in advance by SQA for the material to be read to candidates with additional support needs. The material must be read exactly as printed.

Instructions to reader(s):

The dialogue below should be read in approximately 4½ minutes. On completion of the first reading, pause for two minutes, then read the dialogue a second time.

Where special arrangements have been agreed in advance to allow the reading of the material, those sections marked **(m)** should be read by a male speaker and those marked **(f)** by a female.

Candidates have two minutes to study the questions before the transcript is read.

Alexandra, a German girl, is spending eight months in Scotland.

(m) **Wo wohnst du hier in Schottland?**

(f) Ich wohne in einem kleinen Dorf in Nordostschottland bei einer sehr netten Familie. Meine Eltern und ich hatten von Anfang an ein gutes Gefühl mit der Familie. Ich fühle mich sehr wohl bei der Familie und bin sehr dankbar hier zu sein. Rachel, die Tochter der Familie, ist in der gleichen Klasse hier wie ich.

(m) **Warum wolltest du nach Schottland kommen und hier eine Schule besuchen?**

(f) Ich habe einen Freund, der vor zwei Jahren in Schottland war. In der 11. Klasse in Deutschland gehen viele Schüler ins Ausland. Das Hauptziel für mich nach Schottland zu kommen war es, dass ich Englisch fließend sprechen kann.

(m) **Du bist ja Einzelkind. Wie findest du das?**

(f) Ja, das bin ich. Ich habe keine Brüder oder Schwestern, mit denen ich etwas teilen muss, und das finde ich gut so. Ich kriege die volle Aufmerksamkeit meiner Eltern und das genieße ich sehr.

(m) **Was ist für dich der größte Vorteil des Lebens als Einzelkind?**

(f) Ich bin ja eine ruhige Person, und ich finde es gut, wenn es ruhig bei uns zuhause ist. Ich bin daran gewöhnt, Zeit alleine zu verbringen.

(m) **Hier lebst du in einer Großfamilie. Was sind die Unterschiede?**

(f) Hier in einer Großfamilie zu leben ist ganz anders. Man muss teilen, und es herrscht ein regelrechter Wettbewerb um das Essen—jeder nimmt gleich am Anfang drei Stücke Pizza auf den Teller.

(m) **Wie ist es mit dem Bad, wenn ihr so viele in der Familie seid?**

(f) Wir mussten erstmal darüber sprechen, wann man ins Bad kann. Wir haben es aber hier gut, weil es mehrere Badezimmer gibt.

(m) **Verbringst du Zeit mit deiner Gastfamilie?**

(f) Meine Familie hier ist sehr unternehmungslustig. Sie haben viele Familienfreunde, die oft vorbei kommen, und dann ist das Haus voller Menschen. Manchmal gehen wir auch die Freunde besuchen und verbringen Abende und Nächte, in denen wir Karaoke singen und viel Spass haben. Wir sind zusammen auch schon öfters nach Inverness gegangen, um einzukaufen. Das hat mir auch Spass gemacht.

(m) **Was hat dich hier am meisten überrascht?**

(f) Ich fand es erstaunlich, dass die Schotten im allgemeinen so nett sind. Ich habe es nicht schwer gefunden, mich mit Leuten schnell zu verstehen oder in der Schlange im Supermarkt einfach mal in Gespräche mit fremden Menschen zu kommen.

(m) **Und wie wirst du dich fühlen, wenn du wieder zuhause in Deutschland bist?**

(f) Ich werde natürlich anfangs froh sein, wieder alle meine Freunde zu sehen. Auf der anderen Seite jedoch werde ich mein Leben hier in Schottland schon sehr vermissen. Ich habe dann 8 Monate meines Lebens hier verbracht und mich sehr an den Alltag hier gewöhnt. Es wird seltsam sein, die Menschen hier nicht mehr jeden Tag zu sehen, und ich werde sie alle sehr vermissen.

[END OF TRANSCRIPT]

[BLANK PAGE]

FOR OFFICIAL USE

Examiner's Marks	
A	
B	

Total
Mark

X060/302

NATIONAL
QUALIFICATIONS
2011

THURSDAY, 19 MAY
3.00 PM – 4.00 PM

GERMAN
HIGHER
Listening/Writing

Fill in these boxes and read what is printed below.

Full name of centre

Town

Forename(s)

Surname

Date of birth

Day	Month	Year	Scottish candidate number	Number of seat

Do not open this paper until told to do so.

Answer Section A **in English** and Section B **in German**.

Section A

Listen carefully to the recording with a view to answering, **in English**, the questions printed in this answer book. Write your answers **clearly and legibly** in the spaces provided after each question.

You will have 2 minutes to study the questions before hearing the dialogue for the first time.

The dialogue will be played **twice**, with an interval of 2 minutes between the two playings.

You may make notes at any time but only in this answer book. **Score out any notes before you hand in the book.**

Move on to Section B when you have completed Section A: you will **not** be told when to do this.

Section B

Do not write your response in this book: **use the 4 page lined answer sheet**.

You will be told to insert the answer sheet inside this book before handing in your work.

You may consult a German dictionary at any time during **both** sections.

Before leaving the examination room you must give this book to the Invigilator. If you do not, you may lose all the marks for this paper.

SA X060/302 6/4610

Marks

Section A

Alexandra, a German girl, is spending eight months in Scotland.

1. (*a*) Where in Scotland is Alexandra staying?   1

    (*b*) What does she say about the family she is staying with?   Mention
           three things.   3

2. Why did she want to come to Scotland?   2

3. What does she say about being an only child?   1

4. What is the biggest advantage of life as an only child?   1

5. What are the differences of living in a large family?   3

6. With so many people in the house, what are the arrangements for the
    bathroom?   2

Marks

7. What shows that her Scottish family likes to do lots of things? Mention **three** things.

3

8. What has surprised Alexandra most about the Scots? Mention **two** things.

2

9. How is she going to feel, when she is back in Germany?

2

(20)

[Turn over for Section B on *Page four*

Marks

Section B

Bist du Einzelkind oder kommst du aus einer größeren Familie? Wie kommst du mit deiner Familie aus? Möchtest du das ändern? Warum?

Schreibe 120 – 150 Worte zu diesen Fragen!　　　　　　　　　　**10**

(30)

USE THE 4 PAGE LINED ANSWER SHEET FOR YOUR ANSWER TO SECTION B

[END OF QUESTION PAPER]

[BLANK PAGE]

X060/12/01

NATIONAL QUALIFICATIONS 2012	TUESDAY, 22 MAY 1.00 PM – 2.40 PM	GERMAN HIGHER Reading and Directed Writing

45 marks are allocated to this paper. The value attached to each question is shown after each question.

You should spend approximately one hour on Section I and 40 minutes on Section II.

You may use a German dictionary.

SECTION I—READING

Read the whole of this newspaper article carefully and then answer **in English** the questions which follow it.

Jillian and Danny left home in the US more than a year ago to see the world. They are now in Germany and are staying with Anja, the writer of the article, and her boyfriend in Cologne.

Wenn einer eine Reise tut . . .

Es fing alles im Jahr 2009 an, als mein Freund und ich für unseren Amerika-Urlaub eine Bleibe in *Washington DC* gesucht haben. Über das Internet haben
5 wir Jillian und Danny gefunden. Wir haben sie über die Internetseite von „Couchsurfing" kennen gelernt. Die beiden sind in unserem Alter und haben uns ihre Couch zur Verfügung gestellt.

10 Nach unserem zweitägigen Aufenthalt bei Jillian und Danny war schnell klar, dass die beiden uns auch besuchen kommen sollen. Schon damals spukte eine Idee in den Köpfen der beiden: Eine Reise um
15 die Welt, jeder mit einem Rucksack und dem Nötigsten ausgerüstet—zwei Paar Hosen, drei T-Shirts, Unterwäsche für ein paar Tage, Seife, Shampoo, Zahnbürste, Trinkflasche und Campingausrüstung.
20 Das Badetuch und die Kleidung sind aus Microfaser, schnell trocknend und wasseraufsaugend; alles ist praktisch, schnell waschbar und leicht. Denn das ist das Wichtigste: Alles muss leicht sein.

25 Die beiden haben keinen Zeitdruck auf ihrer Tour. Vor der Abreise haben sie ihren sicheren Job gekündigt. Die Idee ihrer Reise: sich durch nichts und niemanden beeinflussen lassen; einfach zwei Jahre lang
30 leben.

Die Idee dazu hatten die beiden schon früh. Seit dem Collegeabschluss haben sie gespart, um die Reise bezahlen zu können. Außerdem haben sie vor der Abreise
35 die Wohnung und das Auto verkauft, die wichtigsten Sachen bei den Eltern eingelagert, den Rest haben sie verschenkt. Als der Tag der Abreise näher rückte, kam auch die Anspannung und die Frage, ob
40 alles gut gehen wird. „Auf der einen Seite war ich traurig, meine Freunde und Familie

zu verlassen, auf der anderen Seite habe ich mich gefreut, auf eine Weltreise zu gehen", erklärt Jillian.

Von ihrer Heimatstadt flogen sie zuerst 45
nach Mexiko, anschließend nach Mittel- und Südamerika. „Wir haben dort viele Ziele eingeplant", erzählt Danny. „Die eigentliche Herausforderung ist es, mit Enttäuschungen fertig zu werden, 50
besonders wenn etwas nicht so ist, wie man es sich vorgestellt hat."

Nach ihrem neunmonatigen Aufenthalt in Südamerika flogen sie Ende November 2010 zurück nach Hause. „Für uns war 55
es billiger, erst nach Hause zu fliegen und von dort nach Südafrika zu fliegen als von Südamerika nach Südafrika", erklärt Danny. Nach Südafrika reisten sie weiter über Simbabwe, Uganda, und den Nahen 60
Osten nach Deutschland. Danach soll es über Russland nach Asien gehen.

Auf die Frage, was sie nach ihrer Weltreise machen wollen, schauen mich die beiden ratlos an. „Wir haben keine 65
Ahnung," gesteht Danny. Auch Jillian hat noch keine festen Pläne. Vielleicht noch mal studieren oder wieder in den Beruf. „Wir wissen auch noch nicht, in welcher Stadt oder in welchem Staat wir leben 70
werden", sagt Danny.

Eins wissen sie hingegen: Es soll nicht zurück ins alte Leben gehen. „Ich vermisse den Lebensstil, den wir aufgegeben haben, den Fitnessclub, eine gesunde 75
Ernährung, Wochenendausflüge. Aber ich möchte jetzt keinen Job, in dem ich von 9 bis 17 Uhr arbeite und Papier auf dem Schreibtisch herumschiebe", meint Danny. Auch Jillian vermisst die 80
alltäglichen Dinge, die ihr früher auf die Nerven gingen. Wäsche waschen, Essen

kochen, spülen—die tägliche Routine
fehlt ihr.   Aber sie möchte auch nicht
85 missen, was sie alles erfahren und gelernt
hat: „Unsere Beziehung ist anders
geworden, viel enger, weil man die ganze
Zeit zusammen ist", sagt sie.   „In dieser
Situation kann man nicht mehr vor den
Launen des anderen fliehen, sondern muss   90
damit umgehen.   Man kann seine Gefühle
nicht verstecken", klärt Jillian mich auf
und lächelt Danny an.   Schnell sind die
vier Tage vorbei.   Und wieder heißt es
packen, eine Weiterreisemöglichkeit finden,   95
Übernachtungen organisieren.

QUESTIONS

Marks

1. Read lines 1–9.

    (a) How did Anja come to meet Jillian and Danny?   **1**

    (b) What are you told about Jillian and Danny?   **1**

2. Read lines 10–24.

    Why have they chosen to take clothes and towels made of microfibres?

    Mention **four** things.   **2**

3. Read lines 25–30.

    (a) Why is there no time pressure on Jillian and Danny now?   **1**

    (b) What is the idea behind their trip? Mention **two** things.   **2**

4. Read lines 31–44.

    (a) What did they do with all their possessions, before they left America?   **3**

    (b) How did Jillian feel, just before they left?   **2**

5. Read lines 45–52.

    What is the most challenging aspect of the trip?   **2**

6. Read lines 53–62.

    Why did they go back home in November 2010?   **1**

7. Read lines 63–71.

    What are their thoughts and plans for after their world trip? Mention **two** things.   **2**

8. Read lines 72–96.

    (a) What **exactly** does Jillian say is different in their relationship?   **1**

    (b) What are the reasons for this? Mention **two** things.   **2**
    (20)

9. Translate into English:

    „Ich vermisse . . . auf die Nerven gingen. (lines 73–82)   **10**
    (30)

[Turn over for SECTION II on *Page four*

SECTION II—DIRECTED WRITING

Marks

Two years ago you hosted a German student for nine months and last year you were invited by the student's family to spend the entire summer with them; this included going on holiday with them.

When you return to Scotland, you write a report **in German** for the Languages page of your school/college website.

You must include the following information and **you should try to add** other relevant details:

- where in Germany the family live **and** whether you had ever been to Germany before

- what your host family were like **and** how you got on with them

- what you did to help out in the family home

- what you liked about a special outing you went on

- what you found to be different about going away on holiday with a family other than your own one

- whether or not you felt it was a good experience for you to be away from Scotland for such a long time.

(15)

Your report should be 150–180 words in length.

Marks will be deducted for any area of information that is omitted.

[END OF QUESTION PAPER]

X060/12/12

NATIONAL QUALIFICATIONS 2012	TUESDAY, 22 MAY 3.00 PM – 4.00 PM	**GERMAN** HIGHER Listening Transcript

This paper must not be seen by any candidate.

The material overleaf is provided for use in an emergency only (eg the recording or equipment proving faulty) or where permission has been given in advance by SQA for the material to be read to candidates with additional support needs. The material must be read exactly as printed.

> **Instructions to reader(s):**
>
> The dialogue below should be read in approximately 4½ minutes. On completion of the first reading, pause for two minutes, then read the dialogue a second time.
>
> Where special arrangements have been agreed in advance to allow the reading of the material, those sections marked **(m)** should be read by a male speaker and those marked **(f)** by a female speaker.
>
> **Candidates have two minutes to study the questions before the transcript is read.**

Svenja, a German girl, recently spent a year in a school in Britain.

(m)   **In Deutschland wird viel über das Thema Schuluniform diskutiert, weil es bei euch normalerweise so was nicht gibt. Wie siehst du die Sache?**

(f)   Also, ich weiß, dass das Tragen dieser Uniformen in vielen Ländern etwas ganz typisches ist. In Großbritannien und auch in vielen anderen Ländern wie Australien und Neuseeland sind Schuluniformen auch heute noch Pflicht.

(m)   **Du hast neulich ein Jahr in Grossbritannien verbracht und bist dort zur Schule gegangen. Musstest du auch eine Schuluniform tragen?**

(f)   Ja, als Schülerin in England musste ich eine Schuluniform tragen und zwar einen knielangen dunkelblauen Rock, eine weiße Bluse, eine Krawatte und auch einen Blazer mit Schullogo.

(m)   **Hast du deine Schuluniform gerne angezogen?**

(f)   Ja, das hat mich nicht gestört, denn man hat immer die gleichen Sachen an. Man braucht nicht darüber nachzudenken, was man morgens anzieht. Aber bei anderen Mädchen gab es Probleme. Viele haben versucht, aus der Uniform ein individuelles Outfit zu machen.

(m)   **Wie haben sie das gemacht?**

(f)   Sie haben zum Beispiel ihre Röcke kürzer gemacht oder ihre Blazer mit Buttons dekoriert.

(m)   **Und hat es sonst noch Probleme mit der Uniform gegeben?**

(f)   Nicht mit der Uniform selbst, aber andere Schülerinnen haben ziemlich extreme Punkfrisuren getragen oder große Ohrringe.

(m)   **Haben teure Markenklamotten bei dir eine große Rolle gespielt?**

(f)   Na, klar. Wenn ich aus der Schule nach Hause gekommen bin, habe ich mich sofort umgezogen. Das mussten dann schon meine modischen Klamotten sein.

(m)   **Wie war es bei deinen Freundinnen in England?**

(f)   Sie haben sich auch umgezogen, als sie zu Hause angekommen sind. Das Problem aber ist, dass diese Markenklamotten teuer sind. Viele Eltern haben nicht das Geld für diese modischen Sachen.

(m)   **Aber mit der Schuluniform sieht man nicht mehr, wer reiche Eltern hat, oder?**

(f)   Doch, natürlich! Auch mit der Schuluniform sieht man, wer Geld hat und wer nicht. Das fängt schon damit an, dass man die Schuluniform selbst kaufen muss. Manche Schülerinnen müssen die Uniform von einer Schwester oder von einer Cousine nochmals tragen und können auch nicht so oft wechseln, weil sie nur zwei weiße Blusen haben.

(m)   **Und die mit reichen Eltern?**

(f)   Die Mädchen mit reichen Eltern haben vier oder fünf Blusen, die die Mutter jeden Tag bügelt. Da hat man natürlich Unterschiede gesehen. Und diese Unterschiede waren auch allen Leuten klar.

(m)   **Was ist denn eigentlich passiert, wenn man die Uniform einfach nicht angezogen hat?**

(f)   Das gab auf jeden Fall Stress. Man musste sich am nächsten Morgen bei der Schuldirektorin mit Uniform melden. Und wenn man die Uniform nicht anhatte, wurde man nach Hause geschickt, um sich umzuziehen.

(m)   **Nach deinen Erfahrungen in England, glaubst du, dass man auch hier in Deutschland eine Schuluniform einführen sollte?**

(f)   Das kommt darauf an. Die Schüler müssten damit einverstanden sein. Und sie müssten selber entscheiden, wie die Uniform aussieht. Zum Beispiel könnte man nur einen Schulpullover tragen, aber die andere Kleidung selbst wählen.

(m)   **Gibt es schon Schulen in Deutschland, die eine Uniform haben?**

(f)   Ja. In Hamburg gibt es eine Schule mit Uniform. Dort gibt es sogar je nach Jahreszeit verschiedene Uniformen.

[END OF TRANSCRIPT]

[BLANK PAGE]

FOR OFFICIAL USE

Examiner's Marks	
A	
B	

Total
Mark

X060/12/02

NATIONAL
QUALIFICATIONS
2012

TUESDAY, 22 MAY
3.00 PM – 4.00 PM

GERMAN
HIGHER
Listening/Writing

Fill in these boxes and read what is printed below.

Full name of centre

Town

Forename(s)

Surname

Date of birth

Day	Month	Year	Scottish candidate number	Number of seat

Do not open this paper until told to do so.

Answer Section A **in English** and Section B **in German**.

Section A

Listen carefully to the recording with a view to answering, **in English**, the questions printed in this answer book. Write your answers **clearly and legibly** in the spaces provided after each question.

You will have 2 minutes to study the questions before hearing the dialogue for the first time.

The dialogue will be played **twice**, with an interval of 2 minutes between the two playings.

You may make notes at any time but only in this answer book. **Score out any notes before you hand in the book.**

Move on to Section B when you have completed Section A: you will **not** be told when to do this.

Section B

Do not write your response in this book: **use the 4 page lined answer sheet**.

You will be told to insert the answer sheet inside this book before handing in your work.

You may consult a German dictionary at any time during **both** sections.

Before leaving the examination room you must give this book to the Invigilator. If you do not, you may lose all the marks for this paper.

Section A   *Marks*

Svenja, a German girl, recently spent a year in a school in Britain.

1. (*a*) What does Svenja say about the wearing of school uniform in many
        countries?   1

    (*b*) In which **two** countries other than Britain are uniforms compulsory?   1

2. When Svenja was in Britain, what uniform did she have to wear, apart from
    a tie and blazer? Mention **two** things.   2

3. Why did wearing a school uniform not bother her?   2

4. In what ways did some girls try to individualise their school uniforms?   2

5. What steps did other girls take to show their individuality? Mention **one**
    thing.   1

6. To what extent did designer clothes play a role in Svenja's life?   1

Marks

7. What was **one** of the problems that Svenja was aware of with some families and designer clothes?   **1**

8. To what extent do school uniforms still show who has money and who does not?   Mention **two** things.   **2**

9. What does Svenja say about the uniforms of pupils from better-off families?   **2**

10. What happened in her British school, if a pupil arrived at school not wearing uniform?   **2**

11. According to Svenja, what **two** conditions would have to be met, before a school uniform could be introduced in Germany?   **2**

12. What information does Svenja give about the uniform at one school in Hamburg?   **1**

(20)

[Turn over for Section B on *Page four*

Section B *Marks*

Die Uniform in ihrer englischen Schule hat Svenja nicht gestört. Und du, was sind für dich die Vor- und Nachteile einer Schuluniform? Findest du es wichtig, die neueste Mode oder die richtige Marke zu tragen?

Schreibe 120 – 150 Worte zu diesen Fragen! **10**

(30)

USE THE 4 PAGE LINED ANSWER SHEET FOR YOUR ANSWER TO SECTION B

[END OF QUESTION PAPER]

[BLANK PAGE]

Acknowledgements

Permission has been sought from all relevant copyright holders and Bright Red Publishing is grateful for the use of the following:

An article by Sabrina Sodowski taken from the newspaper 'Kölner Stadt-Anzeiger' © Kölner Stadt-Anzeiger (2008 Reading & Directed Writing pages 2 & 3);

The article 'Von Limo zu Sex on the Beach' by Florian Thalmann taken from the newspaper 'Sachsische Zeiturg', Jurge Szene, 16 August 2007 © Sachsische Zeitung GmbH (2009 Reading & Directed Writing pages 2 & 3);

The article 'Neue Heimat' by Andrea Walter taken from 'Brigitte Young Miss', November 2005 © G+J Women New Media GmbH (2010 Reading & Directed Writing pages 2 & 3);

The article 'Hinter den Kulissen des Tourismus' taken from Kölner Stadt-Anzeiger, 23 July 2009 © Kölner Stadt-Anzeiger (2011 Reading & Directed Writing pages 2 & 3);

The article 'Wenn einer eine Reise tut…' taken from the newspaper Kölner Stadt-Anzeiger © Kölner Stadt-Anzeiger (2012 Reading & Directed Writing pages 2 & 3).

SQA HIGHER GERMAN
2008–2012

SECTION I – READING

1. • study/studies/college/university or apprenticeship/
     train(ing)/further education/become a trainee/learn a trade
     <u>and</u> (if study), what (to study)
   • stay at home or move out/take off/leave (your house/home)/
     go elsewhere <u>and</u> (if move out), where (to)

2. (a) • it was the best decision ever/so far/yet
          it was the best decision she ever made
   (b) *Any two from:*
       • she has met/got to know wonderful/great/ marvellous
         people
       • she has experienced (so) many/countless/ numerous/a
         large number of/a lot of new things
         she has had so many new experiences
       • she has become/she is (now) <u>much more</u>
         independent/<u>really</u> independent
       • she has brought/taken/got her English up to a high/
         advanced level/standard

3. (a) *Any two from:*
       • attend/go to college
       • voluntary/charity work
       • language class/course
   (b) • a first-aid course <u>and</u> a Spanish course

4. (a) • meets friends in cafés, to watch videos/films/for a
          video/film evening/movie-night or in a karaoke bar
   (b) • it only takes (about) an hour/it takes (just) under an hour in
          the train to get to New York/Manhattan (from where she
          stays/New Jersey)

5. (a) *Any three from:*
       • <u>family</u> with <u>two</u> hyperactive children
         some families have 2 hyperactive children
       • unfriendly granny lives in the house
         granny who hates young people lives in the house
       • <u>have to/must</u> work until 10.00 pm/22.00 <u>every night</u>
       • only allowed to eat certain things/particular food from
         the fridge
         not allowed particular things to eat from the fridge
   (b) • tiny/small/little room under the stairs

6. (a) • they wanted as little as possible to do with their child(ren)
   (b) • give the 8 year old (boy/son) 70 tablets and/then take the
          boy/child to the psychiatrist

7. *Any two from:*
   • not allowed out during the week/on week-days cannot go
     out during the week/on week-days
     are banned from going out during the week/on week-days
     have a going out ban during the week/on week-days
   • (must) be in/home at/before/by 10.00 pm/22.00 have a
     curfew to be in at 10
     have a 10 pm curfew
   • can stay out/away all night as long as they are back/in/home
     (in time) to waken children
     can stay out all night as long as they wake up the children

8. *Any one from:*
   • be as honest/genuine/truthful as possible
   • think carefully/exactly about what you/to want/expect from
     the year
     consider what you want from the year
   • ask all your questions during the telephone interview
     use a/the telephone interview as an opportunity to put
     questions to the family
     use the telephone interview and ask questions
     have a telephone interview and ask about things

9. *Any two from:*
   • if that is your attitude/in this mind set/in that case/if you
     do,/(because) then hardly anything can go wrong
   • you <u>can</u> <u>look forward</u> to a great/brilliant/fantastic/
     super/mad year
   • new experiences are guaranteed - positive/good as well
     as/and/or negative/bad

10. In meiner Familie bin ich für zwei Schulkinder verantwortlich.
    *In my family I am responsible for/in charge of two
    school-children/school-kids/children of school age*

    Daher habe ich jeden Morgen frei.
    *Because of this/that/For this/that reason/So/That's
    why/Therefore/Hence/This/That means/Due to that I have every
    morning/the morning/(the) mornings/in the morning(s) off/free.
    That's why I am off/free every morning.*

    Am Nachmittag bin ich hauptsächlich dazu da,
    *In the afternoon(s) I am mainly/chiefly here/there
    In the afternoon the main reason I am there is*

    die Kinder zur richtigen Zeit an den richtigen Ort zu bringen
    *to bring/of bringing/(I) bring/to take/of taking/(I) take/to get/of
    getting/(I) get the children to the right/correct/proper place at the
    right/correct/proper time*

    und ihnen am Abend etwas zu kochen.
    *and (to) cook/cooking/(I) cook something for them/them
    something (to eat) in the evening(s).*

SECTION II – DIRECTED WRITING

Please see the table on pages 88–89 which provides details of the
criteria required to produce a good essay answer.

HIGHER GERMAN LISTENING/WRITING 2008

SECTION A

1. *Any three from:*
   - (much) more freedom/freer/more free/more independent
   - can party/celebrate/stay out (with friends) until 3.00 am/the early morning/early in the morning
     can come in at 3.00 am/early in the morning
   - nobody can moan/complain about this/it
   - can have a long lie/stay in bed late/lie in/sleep as long as you want
     can wake/get up when you want
     do not have to get up early
   - can (go and) see/look at what(ever) you want

2. • birthday money from relatives
     or
     saved her birthday money
   • half the money came from parents

3. • (book) flights/flight reservation/plane tickets/plane from Hamburg/plane to Glasgow
   • (book/reserve) bus (tickets) to airport
   • (sort out their) accommodation/youth hostel/somewhere to stay (in Scotland)/place to stay

4. • plane/flight delayed one hour/had to wait an hour for plane to leave
     plane/flight delayed because of fog/(bad) mist/weather
   • one friend/one of the group lost (his) wallet/purse

5. • their room/the room for 5/the room they had booked not available/not free/double-booked
     or
   • they had to find another (youth-)hostel

6. *Any two from:*
   • big/large billiards/snooker/pool room/hall
   • lots of/many/full of games and books
   • barbecue/BBQ in garden
     or
   • small garden

7. • so many shops
     or
   • lot(s) of/many shops in town/city centre

8. • looked at/around/visited/went to see the castle
     or
   • strolled/wandered/meandered along Princes Street
     walked along/up/down Princes Street

9. *Any two from:*
   • rich/strong/wonderful/great culture
     a place of culture/very cultural/lots of culture
   • exciting/good/wicked/buzzing/healthy night-life
   • (very/really) good shopping/shops/shopping possibilities/shopping facilities
     lots of good shops
   • wonderful/beautiful/spectacular/great countryside/nature/scenery/landscape
   • lakes/lochs/Highlands worth seeing

10. • went to Inverness (when she was) in Year 7
    • school/student exchange
      one year Scots go to Hamburg and the next year Germans go to Inverness

11. *Any one from:*
    • get to know/meet new people
    • get to know/meet/discover/experience/learn about/see a different/an exciting/another culture/way of life
    • it was great/really good/lots of fun

SECTION B

Please see the table on pages 91–92 which provides details of the criteria required to produce a good essay answer.

SECTION I – READING

1. (a) *Any one of:*
   - what people/they enjoy about/in the summer (time)
   - people/they love/enjoy/everyone loves the sun, warmth/warm weather/heat and free time in the summer
   - sun, warmth and free time are the best things/their favourite things about summer

   (b) • how people use/spend free/leisure/spare time
   how one uses one's free time
   the use of free time
   what they do/did in their free time

2. (a) • they <u>had to</u>/would/<u>used to</u> walk/run, as there were no buses

   (b) • met/collected/picked up/fetched/got tourists from the ferry went to tourists at the ferry
   - took/carried/brought/dropped off/put their (suit)cases/ luggage/bags to guest houses/B&B/inn/hotel/place they were staying brought their cases to the guest house

   (c) *Any two from:*
   - worked in a milk(-shake) bar/milk-shake shop
   - went walking/hiking <u>a lot</u>/on <u>a lot of</u>/<u>many</u> walks <u>lots of</u> walking tours
   - <u>sometimes</u> went to the Baltic (on holiday).

3. • They took/brought food with them/they took their own food/they had their own food/lunch.
   • If/when they had the money, they bought/would buy <u>a bottle of</u> lemonade/(fizzy-)juice.

4. (a) *Any one of:*
   - They made/sewed/stitched/cut/tailored their own clothes/things.
     Clothes that they altered themselves.
   - Dresses and skirts/a dress and skirt
   - They rolled/bunched/pulled up/folded over/adjusted their skirts to turn them into mini-skirts.
     They wore skirts high as mini-skirts.

   (b) • (They wore) mini-skirts and shorts.
   OR
   • The summer colour was blue.

   (c) *Any one of:*
   - lots of/many colours are fashionable/topical/up-to-date/in fashion/in.
     the current trend is to wear lots of colours.
   - people often wear stripes/stripes are popular/worn a lot/often.
   - lots of colours and stripes.

5. (a) • The only parties were family ones/celebrations.
   Parties were a family thing.
   Parties would be for families.
   There were only family parties.
   They were only at family festivals.
   • The children/young people/you <u>had to</u> be home/in/in the house at/by midnight.
   You <u>had to</u> go back to the house/home by/for midnight.

   (b) • they go to the disco/clubbing/night-clubs <u>every weekend</u>/<u>most weekends</u>/<u>every week</u>/<u>at the weekends</u>.
   • go to/visit town/city festivals/parties/celebrations/ fairs/fêtes/galas/fiestas.

6. • Oma Ingrid – sang hiking/hiker/rambling/walking songs/ they sang songs while they were walking/hiking.
   • Katrin Bredner – they recorded/taped their own voices/ music/tunes (on a cassette recorder) <u>and</u> listened to it.

7. • The sun was very/really important <u>to/for her</u>.
   She found the sun very important.
   • She/you/one could/<u>was able to</u>/<u>got to</u> relax/take it easy/unwind.

8. Wir sind aber nie in den Urlaub gefahren
   But/However/we never/did not ever go/went (away/anywhere)/would never go (away/anywhere)/never used to go (away/anywhere)/on holiday/vacation/for a holiday

   weil wir nicht genug Geld hatten
   because/as/since/we did not have/didn't have/hadn't enough money.

   Meine Mutter sagte oft zu uns Kinder:
   My mother/mum often said/used to say/would say to us children/kids

   „Ich möchte so gerne einmal mit euch in die Bergen fahren…"
   I would/I'd so/really like/I would/I'd so love to go/to travel/to drive/to the mountains with you/one day/some day/sometime/(just) once/.

   Sie wollte uns immer die Alpen zeigen.
   She always wanted/was wanting to show us the Alps.

SECTION II – DIRECTED WRITING

Please see the table on pages 88–89 which provides details of the criteria required to produce a good essay answer.

HIGHER GERMAN
LISTENING/WRITING
2009

SECTION A

1. 4,500

2. (a) • relatively few(er)/only a few/very few/not many/not a lot/too little/very little/hardly any/not very many/not enough for the number of people
fewer/less places than the number of students.

   (b) *Any one from:*
  • to leave/move out of Görlitz/their town/home/parents/ friends.
  • to go to/find/get a place/one in another town/city/ place.
  • to move away/to another town.

3. *Any two from:*
  • not (so) easy.
  • <u>missed</u> her friends/family/home area.
  • knew nobody/did not know anyone.

4. • can bring/take friends home at any time/no matter how late it is/until as late as she wants/when(ever) she wants/at any time of the day/regardless of the time/as late as she likes.
  • <u>at weekend</u> can sleep (in)/lie in/stay in bed as late/long as you want/long lies.
can get up whenever he wants.
sleep all weekend.

5. *Any three from:*
  • You have to/must/having to do everything (for) yourself
She has to/must/having to do everything (for) herself.
  • (You have/she has to do) your/her own shopping/the shopping/buy things for herself/buy everything/shop for herself/pay for her own shopping.
  • (You have) to clean yourself/(she has) to clean herself/do your/her own cleaning/the cleaning/the housework/clean the house.
  • (You have/she has) to budget/make sure money lasts to the end of the month/work out the finances/divide up the money (for the month)/manage your money/keep track of your money/organise your finances for each month.

6. • She is earning/making/earns/gets/makes more money (than friends in Görlitz).
She has been able to earn more money than her friends.
She is better paid in Hamburg.
(You get/earn/make) more money.
Her old friends in Görlitz earn less than her.

7. (*a*) • A colleague/employee/trainee/someone took/was ill.

   (*b*) • She wanted to live/stay in North(ern) Germany.

8. • They went/travelled/came with her to Hamburg.
They went to Hamburg together.
They took her to Hamburg.
  • They looked/searched together/with her for a flat/house/ somewhere to stay/a place to stay/live/accommodation.
They helped her look for/find/get/visit a flat.
They viewed flats with her.
They found a flat with her.
  • They bought her/paid for everything/things/stuff/items/what she needed/everything she needed <u>for the flat/house.</u>
They helped her buy everything <u>for the flat.</u>

9. • Hamburg is (very/so) <u>much/a lot/lots</u> bigger/larger.
One is a big city; the other is a town.
  • The people speak/have/talk a different/their own dialect.
The dialect is different/there are different dialects.
The people speak a different kind of German.

10. *Any one from:*
  • To see/meet (up with)/visit/catch up with her <u>old/childhood</u> friends.
To see the friends she had there.
To see her friends again.

11. • She is <u>more</u> independent/grown-up/self-sufficient/self-reliant/mature.
She is more of an adult.
She has gained in independence.
She can <u>now</u> stand on her own two feet.

SECTION B

Please see the table on pages 91–92 which provides details of the criteria required to produce a good essay answer.

HIGHER GERMAN
READING AND DIRECTED WRITING
2010

SECTION I – READING

1. *Any one from:*
   - To go/be/live somewhere where nobody would know her/ where nobody knew/knows her/who she was
     Because everyone knew her as the minister's daughter
   - As the minister's/priest's/pastor's/vicar's/reverend's daughter you cannot get drunk/let yourself get drunk
   - As the minister's/priest's/pastor's/vicar's daughter you do not want to embarrass your parents

2. (*a*) • People who (would) tell her/explain to her/describe to her what it is like/how it is somewhere else/elsewhere
       • People who tell her what other places are like/what it is like in other places/how other places are/were
         People who tell her how it is living elsewhere

   (*b*) *Any two from:*
       • They vetoed it/they told her she could not go
         They wanted to put a stop to the idea
         They put a veto on it/her
         They tried to veto it/they said she was not allowed
         They put a veto on South Africa
         They exercised their veto/they put a veto in place
         They laid down their veto
         They prohibited her
         They forbad her
         They tried to stop her
       • They were/are worried
         They worried (about it/the idea)
         They worried about her
         They got themselves worried
         It worried them
         They had their worries
       • (They said) the streets are not safe for a woman/girl
         a woman/girl/lady cannot/should not go out in the street
         You cannot go on/into/wander/walk (down) the street(s) as a woman
         It is not a place for women to be alone on the street

3. • (She told them that) they had brought her up/taught her to be independent
     they had taught her independence/to think for herself
     they had made her independent
     they gave her independence
   • Now they were trying/wanting to take an important decision away from her/out of her hands
     Parents wanted to take the decision into their own hands
     They were now trying/wanting to take away her independence
     It was not right that they were trying to take away her independence
     She said did they want to take this important decision out of her hands?

4. • That is her leaving the house/home for ever
     That is her gone for good from home/the house
     She is going to be out of the house for ever
     That's her out of the house for ever
     She has left home for good
     She won't come to live at home again
   • When she comes back, she won't be my little girl anymore
     She will never come back/return as his/my little daughter
     My little girl isn't coming back
     He will never get his little daughter back

   She comes back no more/longer as his little daughter
   She can no longer go back to being his little girl
   She won't come back as his little girl

5. *Any four from:*
   (*a*) • Makes/gets/prepares/cooks breakfast
       Made/got/prepared/cooked breakfast
     • Takes/brings children to school
       Took/brought children to school
     • Goes to fitness studio/gym
       Went to fitness studio/gym
     • Lies in sun/sunbathes/sits in sun
       Lay in sun/sunbathed/sat in sun
     • Reads (a lot)
       Any four for 2 marks; 2 or 3 for 1 mark; less than 2 = 0 marks

   (*b*) • Make/get/give the children/kids a snack/ something to eat
     • Play with the children until the parents come (home/back)/get home/are home/return/arrive

6. (*a*) • Host/Guest father asked his colleague/Karel to take Annette to clubs/to go to clubs with Annette/to go clubbing with Annette
       He was a colleague of the father and the father asked him to take Annette to clubs
     • So that she would see young (life in) Cape Town/ young people's Cape Town
       So that she would see/meet the youth of/young people in Cape Town
       So that she would not be bored

   (*b*) • She wanted/would like to stay there, study there, live/stay/have a life with Karel

7. • To look at/see how she was living/what her lifestyle is
     To see what her life was like
   • (To see) who this guy was who was messing everything up/upsetting everything/the cause of all the confusion/who brought all the confusion/who brought about this muddle/who brought this mess together/who made everything confusing

8. • To apply to study/go to university/college in Cape Town
     To apply for a study/student place in Cape Town
     To apply for her studies in Cape Town

9. • Time will tell where they will end up
     They are leaving (it) open whether to stay in South Africa/ go back to Germany
     They do not know whether they will stay in Cape Town/go back to Germany
     They do not know whether they will leave Cape Town/ stay in Germany
     They will see whether or not they will leave Cape Town/ stay in Germany
   • They have no plans other than/but to enjoy life (now)
     Their only plan is to enjoy life
     No more plans – (to) enjoy life

10. Karel kommt über Weihnachten und Silvester nach Deutschland.
    Karel came/comes to Germany over/for Christmas and New Year/New Year's Eve/Hogmanay/New Years

    Als es Zeit für den Rückflug ist,
    When it was/is time for the flight back/for the return flight/to fly back

    freut sich Annette und ist zugleich sehr traurig.
    Annette was/is happy/glad/pleased/delighted and (yet) (is/was) very sad at the same time/Annette is both happy and very sad at the same time

,,Ich weiß, dass es für meine Familie schwer ist,
I know that it/this is/it's/hard/difficult/tough for/on my family

aber es ist bestimmt die richtige Entscheidung für mich.
but/however it/this is definitely/certainly the right/correct decision for me.

SECTION II – DIRECTED WRITING

Please see the table on pages 88–89 which provides details of the criteria required to produce a good essay answer.

HIGHER GERMAN LISTENING/WRITING 2010

SECTION A

1. (a) • July 2009/last July/<u>almost/nearly</u> a year ago
       Almost a year ago in July

   (b) • 6 weeks

2. • (part-time) job/she has a job/she got a job/she has a wee job
     Savings/she has saved some money
   • Parents (pay the rest)

3. • Had a visit from a cousin from the US
     Cousin from America visited them
     Had a cousin over from the States
     American cousin visited them
   • Told her (a lot) about it/US/the States/America
     Explained/talked about it/US etc.
     Told stories about it/US etc
     Cousin was always talking about it/US etc

4. *Any two from:*
   • You hear so much about it/them
   • Is it like it is in films?/Are they like they are in films?
     She wants to see (for herself) if they are like they are in films
     If the films portray them accurately
     Are the movies accurate?
     She wants to know if everything is really like it looks in the films
   • Is it/school more fun than at home/in Germany?
     School looks more fun than in Germany
     American schools look like fun
     American schools look/seem more fun
     She wants to know if schools are more fun in America
     She feels she will have more fun in school there
     She thinks school in America is more fun than in Germany.
     Wants to see how fun it is compared with her school

5. *Any two from:*
   • Landscape/countryside/scenery
   • Cultural differences
     The differences between the cultures
     The different culture/The culture is different
     Learning about different culture(s)
   • Its/the country's variety
     The (many) different aspects/sides of the country
     The many (different) sides of the country

6. • One hour in <u>car</u>/an hour's <u>drive</u> from Chicago

7. • 11 months
     From August to July

8. (a) • Pleased/happy/glad/delighted/joyful for her
         Happy she is getting such an opportunity
       • It will be hard/difficult (for her)
         She will find it hard when Rica is away
         She will find it hard when she goes
         She will find it hard to cope
         She thinks it will be hard.

   (b) • Good/great that she has this possibility/ opportunity/ chance/ option
         It's a good/great opportunity (for her)
         They are happy that she has this opportunity
         It's good to have the opportunity

9. • Things to remember best friend by
     Things to remind her of best friend
     Keepsake(s)/Memory pieces from her best friend
     Reminders of her best friend

Precious gift from her best friend
Presents/Personal objects from her best friend(s)
- Piano (sheet) music/notes/books/pieces
- German recipes/Granny's recipes

10. • Quite a distance (away)
  (Quite/too/very/rather/really) far (away)
  A long way/journey/distance (away)

11. *Any one from:*
  - More self-confidence/to be more self-confident
    More confident in herself
    More self-assured
  - More independence/to be more independent
    More self-sufficient

SECTION B

Please see the table on pages 91–92 which provides details of the criteria required to produce a good essay answer.

HIGHER GERMAN
READING AND DIRECTED WRITING
2011

SECTION I – READING

1. *Any three from:*
   - Holiday-makers/they sun themselves/bask/sit in the sun/sunbathe/catch/worship the sun/get a tan at/on the square/ in front of/at/outside the/a café
     Must have sun <u>and</u> venue
   - Families coming back from/straight in off the beach/shore
   - (Families/They) have/do not begrudge themselves a cool/cold drink
   - Children have/eat an ice-cream/ice-lolly

2. (a) • People who work/help <u>in the big hotel(s)</u>
       Helpers/Assistants/Workers/Employees/Staff <u>in/from/of (the) big hotel(s)</u>

   (b) • Island 17 kilometres long and a few/not many hundred metres wide
       • Not much work/They don't get a lot of work
         <u>Hotel owner(s)</u> live(s) off summer income
       • Children have to go to mainland/leave the island for (secondary/grammar/higher) school(ing)/education
       • In medical emergencies/For medical assistance reliant/you have to rely on/fly by/be airlifted by helicopter
         The medical problems rely on emergency helicopters
         Medical provision in an emergency depends on a helicopter
         Medical supplies/provisions provided/brought by helicopter in an emergency
         Emergencies have to be taken by helicopter

3. • long white sand(y) beach(es)/shores
     long stretch/strips of white sand
     walk along/absorb long white sandy beaches
   • (good) sea(side)/ocean air/breeze free of/without/away from car/exhaust fumes/emissions/gas(es) from cars/car pollution/car exhaust/car fumes
     The smell of the sea without the smell of car exhaust fumes
     Take in the good sea air instead of car fumes
     Clean sea air because it is not polluted by cars
     Good smell of the sea and not car exhaust fumes

4. (a) • She was the only temp/seasonal/part-time worker in the café
       She was the only helper/assistant in the café

   (b) *Any one from:*
       • Someone else <u>the same age</u> came/another person h<u>er age/of similar age</u> came/followed/ joined
         Another girl <u>her age</u> joined the café to help out
         She got to know/found/met/got a colleague <u>of the same age</u>.
       • She learned/found out that a lot of young people/teenagers/youths from elsewhere/outside the island/out-of-town worked on the island/there
         She learned that a lot of foreign young people worked on the island

   (c) • The locals/residents/islanders/natives went to the same bars/pubs as the holiday-makers/people on holiday
       Inhabitants, visitors and temporary workers all met there/You can meet everyone there/The variety of people that went there all the time

5. (a) • Cups/Mugs and glasses fell off her tray/A cup/mug and glass fell off her tray
     She dropped/broke cups/mugs and glasses off her tray.

    (b) • She wanted to cash up at one table but did not look at the bill
      She tried to charge the wrong customer for 11 beers/She charged someone for beer they did not drink
      She gave the wrong bill (to a/the customer)
      She mixed up table numbers when giving the bill

6. • They were not sympathetic/did not show any understanding/had little understanding/sense/did not understand/did not care about when/that the café wanted to close/it was closing time/they were about to close/they were about to shut the café
   • They do not understand…
     …that the staff want/long to go home after working a 12 hour shift
     …that the staff couldn't wait to stop work after 12 hours
     …that the staff want to see/yearn for an end to their 12 hour working day
     …that they had had enough after working 12 hours
     …that the staff work 12 hour shifts and that it is their time to stop work

7. (a) • She can guess/predict what they are going to order/She knows their order before they say it/ She gets to know what they order/She can, after they have been back several times, order for them/You know what they order/She remembers their orders
     • the nice/friendly/good conversations/chat(s)/talk/ discussion (with them)

    (b) • The ones who cannot/will not/would not/do not want to wait 10 minutes for a coffee/to be served

8. Für uns bedeutet das: Hektik.
For/To us/ourselves
that/this/it means/signifies/represents
meant/signified/represented
it/that means/meant this:

For us that means one thing:
That is what it means for us:

(a) hectic pace/atmosphere.
(a) hectic rush(es).
a hectic time/hectic times
(a) mad rush.
hustle and bustle

For us that means (that) it is (going to be) hectic.

That means a mad rush for us.

Bestellungen aufnehmen und servieren,
Taking (down/in) orders
Record(ing)

and serving them/orders
Taking and serving orders
Orders to take and serve
To take and serve orders
Orders (have) to be taken and served.
Orders are taken and served.
Take a note of orders and serve them.
Take/taking (a note of) orders and serve/serving
We have to take and serve orders

nebenbei den Spülberg in Zaum halten
(whilst) at the same time
at the same time as
(and) in addition/additionally

besides/alongside/along with
as well as/incidentally
while/whilst (also)

(having) to keep/keeping

in check/under control
a check on/check of/control of
on top of/up with
up to date with/a tight rein on

staying in control of/on top of/up to date with

the pile(s)/mountain(s)/heaps of dishes
the pile/mountain of washing-up
the pile of dish-washing

needs to be kept in check

und zwischendurch Geschenke aus dem Souvenirladen einpacken
and

in between times/this/that
between times/that/this
occasionally
in between
between all of that
meanwhile/in the meantime

wrap/wrapping (up)
pack/packing (up)
package/packaging
having to wrap/pack(age)
we/I have to wrap/pack(age)
the wrapping of

presents/gifts

from/out of the souvenir shop
the souvenir shop gifts

– nach solchen Tagen bin ich abends todmüde ins Bett gefallen.
after/on days/a day like this/that
after/on such days/such a day
after these/those days
after these kinds of days/this kind of day

I fell into (my) bed
I would fall into bed
I dropped into bed

in the evening(s)
at night
by the evening
of an evening

dead beat
dead(ly) tired
totally tired
so/very tired
(completely)exhausted
(totally/absolutely) shattered

SECTION II – DIRECTED WRITING

Please see the table on pages 88–89 which provides details of the criteria required to produce a good essay answer.

HIGHER GERMAN LISTENING/WRITING 2011

SECTION A

1. (a) • (little) village in north-east

   (b) *Any threee from:*
   - Very/Really nice
   - (Parents and she) had a good feeling/felt good about the family/Good feeling between the families/Parents were happy to let her stay with them
   - Feels good/happy/is comfortable with the family/She gets on well with them/She feels at home with the family/They make her feel comfortable/She has a good relationship with them/The family is/are hospitable
   - Daughter is in the same class(es)/year

2. *Any two from:*
   - A friend was there two years ago
   - Class/year 11 pupils go abroad/to foreign/different/other countries
   - Can speak English fluently/Wants to speak English fluently/Wants to improve her English/So she could learn better English/So she can practise her English/So that she can make her English flow

3. *Any one from:*
   - Does not <u>have/need</u> to share with brothers/sisters/siblings/anyone/Does not <u>have/need</u> to share things/anything
   - Gets/enjoys full attention of parents/Gets/Has parents all to herself/Parents' attention is never divided

4. *Any one from:*
   - The house is quiet/peaceful/She is a quiet/peaceful person and likes a quiet house/She enjoys the peace when she is home alone/It is quieter in the house which is good Quiet person — quiet house/A quiet household suits her
   - She is used to spending time alone

5. • You/They <u>have to/must/need</u> to share/One/She has to share (a room/at dinner-time)
   - Competition for food/when eating food/Mealtimes are a competition
   - Everyone takes 3 pieces of pizza at the start/at once/You have to take 3 pieces of pizza quickly

6. • Discuss/Agree/Talk about/(Pre-)Arrange when you/each person can use it/have the bathroom/toilet/have a bath Discuss who will use the bathroom first/Everyone has to decide when they will use the bathroom/Arrange who goes first
   - There are several/more/many/multiple bathrooms/There is more than 1 bathroom

7. *Any three from:*
   - They have lots of friends who drop in/visit/come over/come round
     The house is full of people as they have lots of friends
     They have lots of friends so the house is always busy
   - (Go to) visit friends
   - Spend <u>evenings/nights</u> singing/doing karaoke/having fun
   - Go to Inverness shopping (often)

8. *Any two from:*
   - They are so/very nice/kind/friendly/How nice they are
   - Not difficult to get on/along with people
     Gets along well with people/Finds it easy to get on with people
   - (Not difficult) to talk to strangers/people in supermarket (queue)
     If you are in the queue, they are friendly to you
     In the supermarket they talk to strangers

9. *Any two from:*
   - Happy/Glad/Good/Pleased/Excited/Can't wait to see her friends/She will enjoy seeing her friends/Looking forward to seeing her friends/Glad to be back with her family and friends
   - Will miss life in Scotland/the people/her Scottish family/her friends here
   - It will be strange/funny not to see the people here every day

SECTION B

Please see the table on pages 91–92 which provides details of the criteria required to produce a good essay answer.

HIGHER GERMAN READING AND DIRECTED WRITING 2012

SECTION 1 – READING

1. (*a*) • Via/through/over/on the Internet
        On the Internet page of *Couchsurfing*
        Via the Couchsurfing website
        They were looking for somewhere to stay in Washington DC and met them on the Internet.

   (*b*) *Any one from:*
        • They are the same age as the writer/Anja.
          They are in the same age-group/range as Anja.
          They are a similar age to Anja.
          They are the same age as us.

        • They gave Anja (and her boyfriend) a couch to sleep on
          Their couch was available
          They have a couch at their disposal
          They have their couches to offer
          Anja and boyfriend stayed/slept on their couch

2. *Any four from:*
   • They dry (more) quickly/fast(er)/are (more) quick drying/quick to dry.
   • They absorb/soak up (more) water/
     They are (more) (water)- absorbent/They suck up (more) water.
   • (Everything/It is/They are) (more) practical/handy
   • It washes (more) quickly/(more) quickly washable/can be washed (more) quickly/quick(er) to wash/ /they wash fast(er).
   • It is light(er)/(more) lightweight/light(er) material
     It makes their luggage lighter.
   Any 4 for two marks; 2 or 3 for one mark.

3. (*a*) • **Before they left** they gave up/resigned from/quit/left their (secure) jobs/gave/handed in their notice.

   (*b*) • To be influenced by nothing/nobody.
          No person/thing should/to influence them.
          To be under nobody's influence/With nobody to influence them/Nobody will be able to influence them.
          To stop being influenced by anyone.
          So that nobody could influence what they were doing.
          Without any outside pressure or influence.

        • Simply/Just (want) to live for two years
          To live this way for 2 years
          Simply 2 years of living
          This was 2 years simply to <u>live/just</u> to live.
          They are going to live their own way for 2 years.
          Simply to have 2 years to themselves

4. (*a*) • They sold their flat/apartment/house/accommodation **and** car.

        • They stored the (most) important/valuable things/stuff with their parents/at their parents'.
          They gave the (most) important things to their parents to store/to look after.
          They left/kept the (most) important things with their parents/at their parents'.

        • They gave the rest/everything else/the remainder away/to other people.
          They gifted the rest to other people.

   (*b*) • (On the one hand) sad to be leaving **friends and family**
          Sad - she would miss her **friends and family**

        • (On the other hand) pleased/delighted/thrilled/excited/happy/joyful/glad/looking forward to be going on a world trip/tour/to be going round the world/to see the world

5. • Coming to terms/Coping/Having to deal with/Getting over disappointment(s)/being disappointed/To be rid of feelings of disappointment

   • (Especially/Particularly) if/when something is not as/what/how they/you expected/imagined
     If something is not like the expectations you had
     If something does/did not live up to expectations
     If something is different from the expectations/what they thought it was going to be

6. • It was cheaper to fly/go home first and then fly to South Africa than to fly from South America to South Africa.
     Cheaper to fly to South Africa from their home country/home than from South America to South Africa.
     More expensive to fly direct from South America to South Africa than to fly home first then to South Africa.

7. *Any two from:*
   • They do not/Danny does not have a clue.
     They have no idea.
     They have/Jillian has no **fixed/firm/solid/definite** plan(s).

   • Study **or** return to their careers/occupation/resume her/their occupation/start their career again/return to their job
     Study **or** continue with their career/work/Go in to their profession again

   • They don't (even) know what town or state they will/want/are going to live in.
     They are not sure what town or state they will live in.
     They need to decide what town or state they will live in.

8. (*a*) • Relationship/It is (a lot) closer/tighter/They have a (much) tighter relationship/They are (a lot) closer/ They have become (a lot/much) closer…
          … as/because they are together all the time/the whole time/because of all the time they spent together/because they were together all the time.

   (*b*) • They/You cannot run/get away/escape/flee from each other's moods/if one (of them/you) is in a mood/the other person's moods

          They/You have to learn how to cope/deal with/work through/handle each other's moods.
          You have to learn how to cope when one is in a mood.
          You have to face them and learn how to deal with them.

        • They cannot hide (their) feeling(s).
          You cannot hide (your) feeling(s).

9. „Ich vermisse den Lebensstil, den wir aufgegeben haben,
   "I miss

   the lifestyle
   the style/way of life

   that/which
   omission of "that/which"

   we have given up
   we gave up

den Fitnessclub, eine gesunde Ernährung, Wochenendausflüge.
the fitness club/centre/studio
the leisure club/centre/studio
the gym

a healthy diet
eating healthy/healthily
healthy eating/nutrition
healthy nourishment
(eating) healthy food
a healthy way of eating
healthy eating habits

Ignore addition of 'and'

weekend trips.
weekend outings.
weekend excursions.
outings/trips/excursions at the weekend.

Aber ich möchte jetzt keinen Job, in dem ich von 9 bis 17 Uhr arbeite
But/However

I wouldn't/would not like (to have) a/any job
I would not want a/any job
I would like no job

now

in which
where

I am working
I work
I worked/were working

(from) 9 (am) to 5 (pm)
(from) 9 (am) till/until 5 (pm)
From 9 to 5 o'clock

But I would like to have no job now where I am working from 9 to 5.

und Papier auf dem Schreibtisch herumschiebe", meint Danny.
and

push
move
shove
(pushing/moving/shoving – following on from earlier sections)

paper/papers

around the/my (writing) desk,"
round on the/my desk,"

push around paper(s) on the/my desk,"

says/states/thinks/opines Danny.
said/stated/thought/opined Danny.

Auch Jillian vermisst die alltäglichen Dinge, die ihr früher auf die Nerven gingen.
Jillian too/also
Also Jillian

misses

the everyday things
the day-to-day things
the ordinary/routine things

which/that

got/have got on her nerves
annoyed/have annoyed her
irritated/have irritated her
got her annoyed

before/previously/formerly
in the past/earlier

which used to get on her nerves.
which had previously annoyed her.
which once got on her nerves.

SECTION II – DIRECTED WRITING

Category	Mark	Content	Accuracy	Language Resource – Variety, Range, Structures
Very Good	15	• All bullet points are covered fully, in a balanced way, including a number of complex sentences. • Some candidates may also provide additional information. • A wide range of verbs/verb forms, tenses and constructions is used. • Overall this comes over as a competent, well thought-out account of the event which reads naturally.	• The candidate handles all aspects of grammar and spelling accurately, although the language may contain some minor errors or even one more serious error. • Where the candidate attempts to use language more appropriate to post-Higher, a slightly higher number of inaccuracies need not detract from the overall very good impression.	• The candidate is comfortable with almost all the grammar used and generally uses a different verb or verb form in each sentence. • There is good use of a variety of tenses, adjectives, adverbs and prepositional phrases and, where appropriate, word order. • The candidate uses co-ordinating conjunctions and subordinate clauses throughout the writing. • The language flows well.
Good	12	• All bullet points are addressed, generally quite fully, and some complex sentences may be included. • The response to one bullet point may be thin, although other bullet points are dealt with in some detail. • The candidate uses a reasonable range of verbs/verb forms and other constructions.	• The candidate generally handles verbs and other parts of speech accurately but simply. • There may be some errors in spelling, adjective endings and, where relevant, case endings. • Use of accents may be less secure. • Where the candidate is attempting to use more complex vocabulary and structures, these may be less successful, although basic structures are used accurately. • There may be minor misuse of dictionary.	• There may be less variety in the verbs used. • The candidate is able to use a significant amount of complex sentences. • In one bullet point the language may be more basic than might otherwise be expected at this level. • Overall the writing will be competent, mainly correct, but pedestrian.
Satisfactory	9	• The candidate uses mainly simple, more basic sentences. • The language is perhaps repetitive and uses a limited range of verbs and fixed phrases not appropriate to this level. • In some examples, one or two bullet points may be less fully addressed. • In some cases, the content may be similar to that of good or very good examples, but with some serious accuracy issues.	• The verbs are generally correct, but basic. • Tenses may be inconsistent, with present tenses being used at times instead of past tenses. • There are quite a few errors in other parts of speech – personal pronouns, gender of nouns, adjective endings, cases, singular/plural confusion – and in the use of accents. • Some prepositions may be inaccurate or omitted eg I went the town. • While the language may be reasonably accurate in three or four bullet points, in the remaining two control of the language structure may deteriorate significantly. • Overall, there is more correct than incorrect.	• The candidate copes with the past tense of some verbs. • A limited range of verbs is used to address some of the bullet points. • Candidate relies on a limited range of vocabulary and structures. • Occasionally, the past participle is incorrect or the auxiliary verb is omitted. • Sentences may be basic and mainly brief. • There is minimal use of adjectives, probably mainly after "is" eg The boss was helpful. • The candidate has a weak knowledge of plurals. • There may be several spelling errors eg reversal of vowel combinations.

Category	Mark	Content	Accuracy	Language Resource – Variety, Range, Structures
Unsatisfactory	6	• In some cases the content may be basic. • In other cases there may be little difference in content between Satisfactory and Unsatisfactory. • The language is repetitive, with undue reliance on fixed phrases and a limited range of common basic verbs such as *to be, to have, to play, to watch*. • While the language used to address the more predictable bullet points may be accurate, serious errors occur when the candidate attempts to address the less predictable areas. • The Directed Writing may be presented as a single paragraph.	• Ability to form tenses is inconsistent. • In the use of the perfect tense the auxiliary verb is omitted on a number of occasions. • There may be confusion between the singular and plural form of verbs. • There are errors in many other parts of speech – gender of nouns, cases, singular/plural confusion, spelling and, where appropriate, word order. • Several errors are serious, perhaps showing mother tongue interference. • There may be one sentence which is not intelligible to a sympathetic native speaker. • One area may be very weak. • Overall, there is more incorrect than correct.	• The candidate copes mainly only with the predictable language required at the earlier bullet points. • The verbs "was" and "went" may also be used correctly. • There is inconsistency in the use of various expressions, especially verbs. • Sentences are more basic. • An English word may appear in the writing or a word may be omitted. • There may be an example of serious dictionary misuse.
Poor	3	• The content and language may be very basic. • However, in many cases the content may be little different from that expected at Unsatisfactory or even at Satisfactory.	• Many of the verbs are incorrect or even omitted. • There are many errors in other parts of speech – personal pronouns, gender of nouns, adjective endings, cases, singular/plural confusion, word order, spelling. • Prepositions are not used correctly. • The language is probably inaccurate throughout the writing. • Some sentences may not be understood by a sympathetic native speaker.	• The candidate cannot cope with more than 1 or 2 basic verbs, frequently *had* and *was*. • The candidate displays almost no knowledge of past tenses of verbs. • Verbs used more than once may be written differently on each occasion. • The candidate has a very limited vocabulary. • Several English or "made-up" words may appear in the writing. • There are examples of serious dictionary misuse.
Very Poor	0	• The content is very basic OR • The candidate has not completed at least three of the core bullet points.	• (Virtually) nothing is correct. • Most of the errors are serious. • Very little is intelligible to a sympathetic native speaker.	• The candidate copes only with "have" and "am". • Very few words are correctly written in the foreign language. • English words are used. • There may be several examples of mother tongue interference. • There may be several examples of serious dictionary misuse.

HIGHER GERMAN
LISTENING/WRITING
2012

SECTION A

1. (a) • It is (quite) typical/normal/It exists.
          It is common./It belongs to daily life.

   (b) • Australia **and** New Zealand

2. *Any two from:*
   • Knee-length skirt
   • Dark/navy-blue (skirt)
   • White blouse/shirt

3. • You all/always have the **same** things on/wear
     the **same** things.
     Everyone wears the **same** things/had the **same** clothes.
     Everyone is/looks/dresses the **same**.
     Everyone was/dressed/looked the **same**.
     It was the **same** clothes every day.

   • You don't need to think about/choose/decide/worry
     about/organise/plan/pick out what to put on/wear.

4. • They made/make their skirt(s) short(er)/shortened their
     skirts/rolled up their skirt(s).

   • They decorated their blazer(s) with badges/pins.
     They put/stick/wore badges/pins on their blazers/pins.
     Blazers with badges/pins

5. *Any one from:*
   • (They had) extreme/punk hair-styles/haircuts
     Exaggerated hair-style/Extreme haircuts/hair colours

   • (They wore) big/large/huge ear-rings

6. • She changed into them/her fashion gear/fashionable clothes
     as soon as/when she got home.
     She (always) wears them at home.
     After school she changes into them.
     Only when she got home from school.
     She wears them when not in school.
     When she came home she had to be in her designer clothes.

7. • They did/do not have the/enough money for them.
     They cost too much./They are too dear.
     They cannot afford them.
     They are/were not cheap.
     (They are) expensive.
     The cost

8. • Hand-me-downs – Any response which shows an
     understanding of getting clothes worn by another member
     of the family e.g.
     Some pupils have to wear a uniform they got from their
     sister or cousin.

   • They/The poorer ones only have/can only afford two (white)
     blouses/shirts.
     People with rich parents have more blouses/shirts.
     The poorer ones cannot change as often.

9. • They have 4 or 5 blouses/shirts/tops
     They have 4/5 blouses/shirts

   • Which mother irons **every day**
     Which mother **always** ironed
     Which are **always** ironed

10. • Had to report to/meet with/see head teacher/rector/director/
      principal/headmaster/headmistress **next morning/day**.
      Got spoken to by headteacher **the next day**.

    • (If no uniform,) sent home **to change**.

11. • Pupils/Kids (would have to) **agree** to it/having a uniform/
      pullover/jumper/sweater.
      Pupils would have to think it was OK.

    • They/The school would have to/must decide themselves
      what the uniform should be/look like/ what was part of the
      uniform.
      They have to agree on a style.

      Not a whole uniform, just a pullover
      Introduce uniform slowly by wearing just a pullover
      May have to introduce a school jumper before other uniform
      You could wear a school jumper but choose other clothes
      yourself
      Try just one item e.g. a jumper
      Start with a pullover

12. • (Different) uniform for each season/according to the
      season/time of year
      One for each season/time of year

SECTION B

Category	Mark	Content	Accuracy	Language Resource – Variety, Range, Structures
Very Good	10	• The topic is covered fully, in a balanced way, including a number of complex sentences. • Some candidates may also provide additional information. • A wide range of verbs/verb forms and constructions is used. There may also be a variety of tenses. • Overall this comes over as a competent, well thought-out response to the task which reads naturally.	• The candidate handles all aspects of grammar and spelling accurately, although the language may contain some minor errors or even one more serious error. • Where the candidate attempts to use language more appropriate to post-Higher, a slightly higher number of inaccuracies need not detract from the overall very good impression.	• The candidate is comfortable with almost all the grammar used and generally uses a different verb or verb form in each sentence. • There is good use of a variety of tenses, adjectives, adverbs and prepositional phrases and, where appropriate, word order. • The candidate uses co-ordinating conjunctions and subordinate clauses throughout the writing. • The language flows well.
Good	8	• The topic is addressed, generally quite fully, and some complex sentences may be included. • The candidate uses a reasonable range of verbs/verb forms and other constructions.	• The candidate generally handles verbs and other parts of speech accurately but simply. • There may be some errors in spelling, adjective endings and, where relevant, case endings. • Use of accents may be less secure. • Where the candidate is attempting to use more complex vocabulary and structures, these may be less successful, although basic structures are used accurately. • There may be minor misuse of dictionary.	• There may be less variety in the verbs used. • Most of the complex sentences use co-ordinating conjunctions, and there may also be examples of subordinating conjunctions where appropriate. • At times the language may be more basic than might otherwise be expected at this level. • Overall the writing will be competent, mainly correct, but pedestrian.
Satisfactory	6	• The candidate uses mainly simple, more basic sentences. • The language is perhaps repetitive and uses a limited range of verbs and fixed phrases not appropriate to this level. • The topic may not be fully addressed. • In some cases, the content may be similar to that of good or very good examples, but with some serious accuracy issues.	• The verbs are generally correct, but basic. • Tenses may be inconsistent. • There are quite a few errors in other parts of speech – personal pronouns, gender of nouns, adjective endings, cases, singular/plural confusion – and in the use of accents. • Some prepositions may be inaccurate or omitted eg I go the town. • While the language may be reasonably accurate at times, the language structure may deteriorate significantly in places. • Overall, there is more correct than incorrect and there is the impression overall that the candidate can handle tenses.	• The candidate copes with the present tense of most verbs. • A limited range of verbs is used. • Candidate relies on a limited range of vocabulary and structures. • Where the candidate attempts constructions with modal verbs, these are not always successful. • Sentences may be basic and mainly brief. • There is minimal use of adjectives, probably mainly after "is" eg My friend is reliable. • The candidate has a weak knowledge of plurals. • There may be several spelling errors eg reversal of vowel combinations.

Category	Mark	Content	Accuracy	Language Resource – Variety, Range, Structures
Unsatisfactory	4	• In some cases the content may be basic. • In other cases there may be little difference in content between Satisfactory and Unsatisfactory. • The language is repetitive, with undue reliance on fixed phrases and a limited range of common basic verbs such as *to be, to have, to play, to watch*. • While the language used to address the more predictable aspects of the task may be accurate, serious errors occur when the candidate attempts to address a less predictable aspect. • The Personal Response may be presented as a single paragraph.	• Ability to form tenses is inconsistent. • In the use of the perfect tense the auxiliary verb is omitted on a number of occasions. • There may be confusion between the singular and plural form of verbs. • There are errors in many other parts of speech – gender of nouns, cases, singular/plural confusion – and in spelling and, where appropriate, word order. • Several errors are serious, perhaps showing mother tongue interference. • There may be one sentence which is not intelligible to a sympathetic native speaker. • Overall, there is more incorrect than correct.	• The candidate copes mainly only with predictable language. • There is inconsistency in the use of various expressions, especially verbs. • Sentences are more basic. • An English word may appear in the writing or a word may be omitted. • There may be an example of serious dictionary misuse.
Poor	2	• The content and language may be very basic. • However, in many cases the content may be little different from that expected at Unsatisfactory or even at Satisfactory.	• Many of the verbs are incorrect or even omitted. • There are many errors in other parts of speech – personal pronouns, gender of nouns, adjective endings, cases, singular/plural confusion – and in spelling and word order. • Prepositions are not used correctly. • The language is probably inaccurate throughout the writing. • Some sentences may not be understood by a sympathetic native speaker.	• The candidate cannot cope with more than 1 or 2 basic verbs, frequently "has" and "is". • Verbs used more than once may be written differently on each occasion. • The candidate has a very limited vocabulary. • Several English or "made-up" words may appear in the writing. • There are examples of serious dictionary misuse.
Very Poor	0	• The content is very basic	• (Virtually) nothing is correct. • Most of the errors are serious. • Very little is intelligible to a sympathetic native speaker.	• The candidate copes only with "have" and "am". • Very few words are correctly written in the foreign language. • English words are used. • There may be several examples of mother tongue interference. • There may be several examples of serious dictionary misuse

Hey! I've done it

iBrightRED
PUBLISHING

© 2012 SQA/Bright Red Publishing Ltd, All Rights Reserved
Published by Bright Red Publishing Ltd, 6 Stafford Street, Edinburgh, EH3 7AU
Tel: 0131 220 5804, Fax: 0131 220 6710, enquiries: sales@brightredpublishing.co.uk,
www.brightredpublishing.co.uk

Official SQA answers to 978-1-84948-289-9
2008-2012